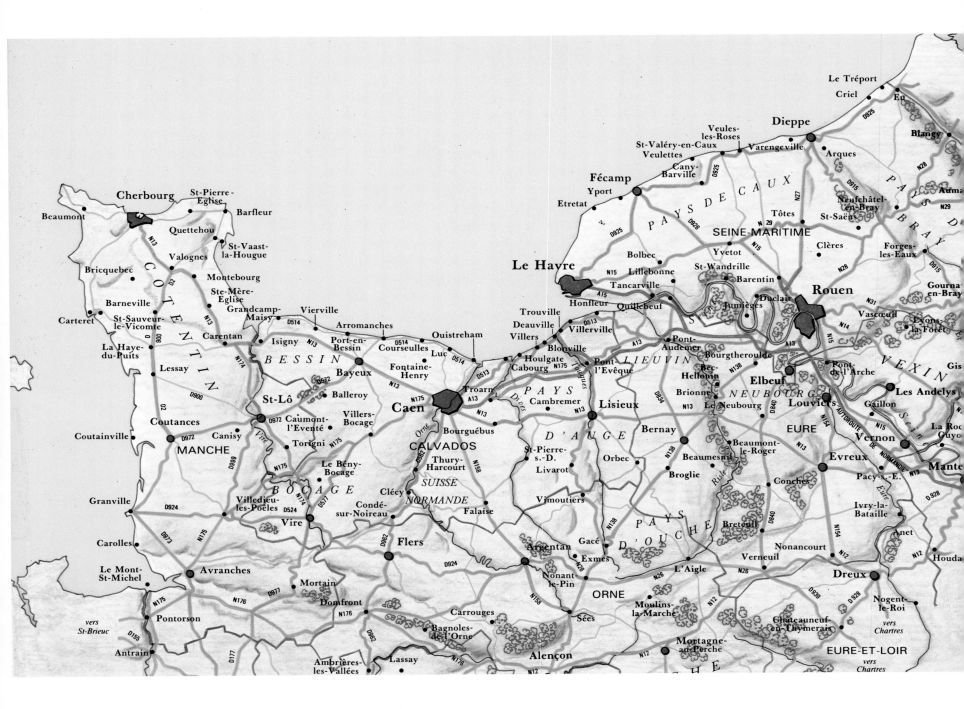

Cover photographs:
*Coupesarte's manor house in the Auge region, detail of Notre-Dame cathedral in Rouen,
the cliffs at Etretat, Saint-Hippolyte's manor house.*

Back cover:
Apple-trees in blossom in the Auge region and the Mont-Saint-Michel.

THE ENCHANTING
NORMANDY

Text Noël Graveline

minerva

Table of contents

VERNON AND ITS SURROUNDINGS

Rustic wardrobes decorated with character, timbered houses, the shade of the apple trees dotted about the broad pastures – this, together with a mosaic of fields through which the languid Seine winds its dignified way, and also a sky whose subtle variations proved so challenging to the Impressionists…

More than anything else, Normandy, quite apart from its popular image, offers the visitor a range of elusive nuances – so much so that the word "impressions" perhaps best conveys the nature of its personality. In fact the painting by Claude Monet bearing that name, and which was to launch the artistic world towards new horizons was painted at Le Havre. In Rouen the paintings by the precursor of Impressionism captured the fleeting half-light of the cathedral; indeed Monet chose to spend the more fruitful half of his life here, between the sky and the water of Normandy.

Well away from Le Havre, Normandy's oceangoing port where he had spent his childhood and acquired his fondness for seascapes, Monet focussed on those places which bore the imprint of the early history of the province, at the borders of Ile-de-France. His renown came to be associated with the small town of Giverny, near Vernon at the confluence of the Epte and Seine, home of the real life picture that Monet considered to be his masterpiece, the famous water garden later immortalized in the Water Lilies series. The pink hillside mansion with green shutters, in which the painter settled in 1883, has been

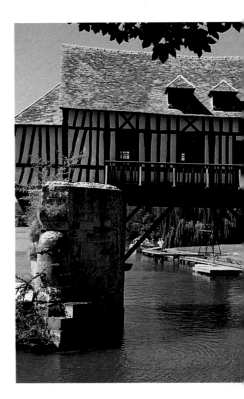

diligently restored, and now houses a national museum where the visitor will find a wonderful complement to the great exhibitions in Paris. The gardens, rather than the reproductions of famous paintings or the painter's studios or everyday objects, tell us most about Monet's creative quest, which triggered an extraordinary pictorial movement in Normandy, the land of shimmering light. In order not to miss a single one of those fascinating vibrations, the artist, who used to rent bales of straw from nearby farmers, in order to scrutinize as closely as possible the effects produced on their bulk by sunlight, decided to set up, on his own doorstep an environment rich enough for his own palette. The result was the Clos Normand, with its profusion of flowers, and, on the other side of a tunnel, the Japanese garden,

a worthy appendage of his superb collection of engravings. For this purpose he had dug out a pond and diverted a branch of the Epte, which still flows beneath the Japanese bridge and its exotic species.

Despite its modest dimensions, the Valley of the Epte is of even greater historical importance than the Valley of the Avre, to the south: it is not only the frontier, but also the birthplace, of the province. The event took place at Saint-Clair-sur-Epte, in the year 911, when Charles the Simple (a nickname meaning "honest" in old French or "sincere" in old French) ceded Neustrie to Rolf the Marcher, chief of the Normans, those "North men" whose bands had ravaged the Seine Valley for a hundred years. The French king hoped that the new duke would be anxious to defend his territory, and

Above and left:
Vernon, the old mill on the Seine.

Left:
*Château-sur-Epte, the ruins
of the castle.*

Previous pages:
*Saint-Hippolyte's manor house,
in the Auge region.*

Above and top:
Claude Monet's house at Giverny

Right, top:
The artist's large studio.

Right, bottom:
The water-lily pond.

that he would thereby protect the kingdom from renewed Viking incursions: his assumption later proved to be correct, as Norman territorial ambitions were assuaged at England's expense. However, what the king failed to foresee was that the power of the dukes of Normandy, thus strengthened by William the Conqueror, would become a threat to the French crown. Thereafter the Epte Valley, strewn with heavily fortified castles, was an increasingly contested frontier.

The town of Vernon, on the Seine just downstream from Giverny, marked the limits of the duchy; it changed hands a number of times, on account of the strategic importance of its bridge. But the military architecture related to those far-off days now has a very discreet presence. On the right bank, Tourelles Castle – guardian of the old bridge, whose first piers are still standing – protrudes from among the greenery of the Vernonnet district. In town one still can see some sections of the ramparts and the Archives Tower, once the keep of the castle. Vernon is also graced by its collegiate church of Notre-Dame, a 12th century structure which, as can be seen from the elegant west door, with its flamboyant rose window, has been much renovated since then, as well as some halftimbered houses, luckily spared by the fighting in 1944. One of them, the former mansion of a local lord, now houses the A.G. Poulain museum, with its interesting collection of works by artists from Giverny. But Vernon owes its appeal less to its architecture than to the charm of its rural setting – a commodity much valued at the outer edges of the Greater Paris area. Here the Seine interrupts its meandering course, flowing instead past long wooded islands, with mature forests on either bank. The star attraction of Vernon Forest is the gigantic Mère-de-Dieu oak tree. Bizy Forest, like Vernon, is also quite extensive, and is named after the château, with its admirable park, standing between it and the town. There are plenty of vantage points, high above the river, which enable one to enjoy this landscape, from Saint-Michel to Le Signal des Coutumes or Notre-Dame-de-la-Mer, where the landscape begins to resemble the cliffs near Les Andelys.

THE SEINE VALLEY, LES ANDELYS, CHÂTEAU-GAILLARD

During the summer months it is possible to embark at Vernon in a motor launch reminiscent of the passenger barges that once competed with the stage coaches between Paris and Rouen.

On the way, as the peaceful landscape slips quietly by, one can try to imagine what Normandy must have been like in the year 1000, and consider the circumstances which caused this colossal fortress to be erected in the first place.

Encouraged by their new legitimate status among the Franks, the Normans under Rol and his successors worked to integrate this southerly into the Scandinavian economy, flourishing at the time. Having readily adopted the Christian religion, following the example set by their chief, whose name changed to Rollo and then to Robert, they rebuilt the buildings that they had left in ruins at the time of the invasions and restored the power of the monasteries. Mont-Saint-Michel and Notre-Dame-de-Rouen are the finest specimens of the religious buildings which flourished so abundantly under the Normans. In particular, this golden

Above:
The Seine Valley, near Les Andelys.

Left:
The abbey of Fontaine-Gérard.

Right:
The church of Pont-de-l'Arche.

age brought the emergence of a new breed of men combining the Viking spirit of conquest and the foundations of French culture. The building of churches was not enough for these men, who once again put to sea in the quest for new kingdoms, this time Sicily, Antioch and England. The dukes of Normandy, vassals of the French king, thus became kings themselves, and defenders of Christianity – despite the fact that their forefathers had been Viking bandits. In this way, around 1190, the Third Crusade was led by Philippe-Auguste and Richard Lionheart, two brave warriors who were also crafty and unscrupulous statesmen, of roughly equal ability. This escapade marked the end of an understanding which was more like a truce. Normandy was clearly to be the prize for which the two sides contended, the king of France wishing to enlarge the possessions of the crown, and Richard being determined to keep control over his domain.

The fighting initially turned to the advantage of Philippe-Auguste who chose to attack Rouen, with the backing of a river-based army. Richard then decided to block his path by

sealing off the entire valley at Le Petit Andely. He drew up plans for a sort of fortified line, modelled on the techniques of warfare he had seen during the Crusades, which would extend the cliff and built a barricade of piles across the river, thus also closing the Bernières Plain. With thousands of workers under his command he stepped up the pace of construction to the point where this presumably impregnable fortress was completed in an exceptionally short time. He exclaimed, when describing his accomplishment, "Look at my beautiful yearling!" Yet two silly mistakes were enough to change the course of history. While out walking carelessly in front of a besieged castle in Limousin, Richard Lionheart was fatally injured by a crossbow; and his successor, Landless John, thoughtlessly had latrines added on the outside of the second surrounding wall – thus providing a weak point through which the daring soldiers of Philippe-Auguste succeeded in taking over the entire fortress. Normandy once again became French; but the same antagonists were to fight over Château-Gaillard once again during the Hundred Years'

War; it figured so prominently in the Wars of Religion – four hundred years after Richard – that Henry IV had it dismantled. Its strategic value is therefore beyond question.

Standing before the outer walls, which in places are more than sixteen feet thick, a student of military architecture can readily appreciate the high quality of the defenses; the castle pointing defiantly, like the prow of a ship, towards Ile-de-France, the protective wall surrounding the bailey, then the massive second line and the embanked keep towering over the cliff. One can still see the governor's residence and the casemates where a stock of supplies was kept to withstand sieges lasting over a year. However, it is the incomparable view of the Seine and Les Andelys that is the most noteworthy feature of Château-Gaillard.

The town, situated at the foot of this remarkable scene is attractive in its own right. One is struck by the contrast between the Gothic elegance of the church of Saint-Sauveur, near the river, and the somewhat more composite majesty of the collegiate church of Notre-Dame, at the other end of the avenue which links Le Petit and Le Grand Andely. This large church, essentially Renaissance in design, commemorates St. Clothilde, Clovis wife; after converting her husband to Catholicism she founded a monastery at this site and, in order to quench the thirst of the masons she changed the water of the fountain into wine. Unfortunately all that remains of the miracle is the reddish color of the water – with a high iron content – and the fine stained-glass windows of the church, which relate this episode in her life.

As the river gradually winds its way downstream, the cliffs gradually give way to low wooded banks; it was in this setting that Richard Lionheart founded Bonport Abbey, whose handsome remains can still be seen. However, the scenery becomes more exciting with the return of steep river banks, and the rugged landscape of La Roque, Saint-Adrien and, above all, the famous Deux Amants Hill, a superb belvedere brings to mind the romantic legend which, since the 12th century, has inspired so many painters and poets.

Above:
*At Les Andelys,
Château-Gaillard.*

Top:
Les Andelys.

Facing page:
*Notre-Dame au Grand-Andely
has a quite remarkable series of
Renaissance stained glass windows.*

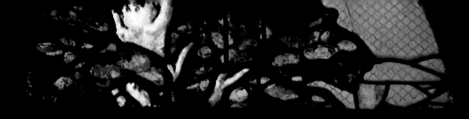

1540

SMOOTH LAND BETWEEN
THE SEINE AND THE EURE

The sight of Château-Gaillard, its proud silhouette standing out beyond the winding course of the Seine, must have played a big part in the decision of Georges d'Amboise, Archbishop of Rouen, to convert for his own use the castle which his predecessors had been given by Saint Louis.

Gaillon, with its admirable location, was remarkably well suited to the ambitions of this cardinal-minister, who was also a papal legate. Gaillon, as the architectural vanguard of the time, marked the abandonment of Gothic ornamentation for the sake of a style which was no mere servile copy of work done in Italy, and which the châteaux of the Loire Valley were to carry to the peak of perfection. A century later, Hardouin-Mansart and Le Nôtre completed this sumptuous palace, that came to be known as the Versailles of the Renaissance.

Whereas Gaillon stands a short distance back from the river, the town of Louviers, near the next loop, lies

wholly within the embrace of the Eure, several of its arms flowing through it, just upstream from the confluence of the two rivers. The town is located in such a delightful and serene natural setting – perhaps at the origin of its Latin name, meaning "sojourn of springtime" – that one can readily see why its founder, a duke of Normandy, had chosen to build his manor here, which had been ceded to the archbishops of Rouen by Richard Lionheart, began to acquire increasing numbers of woolworking draper's shops – this being a traditional activity boosted by Colbert, who installed a royal manufacture at Louviers. The town has recently lost

Above:
View of Gaillon.

Left:
At Moulineaux, the castle of Robert the Devil.

Facing page:
A drakkar, from the Viking museum in the castle.

the last of its textile plants, yet its diversified industrial base was inherited from the 19th century, when factories making carding machines and looms were set up here. Were it not for the damage done in 1940, the heart of the town would have retained its ancien régime character intact. However, although most of the half-timbered houses have disappeared, Notre-Dame still exists; the south porcin of this remarkable church is commonly regarded as the archetypal illustration of Flamboyant Gothic, and has been described as "more the work of jewelers than of masons".

Near the pine groves which lend a Mediterranean air to the confluence of the Eure, we come to the small town of Pont-de-l'Arche, so named because it was the first to have its own bridge over the Lower Seine, at a time when even Rouen lacked such a structure. Before striking out to the north, towards the great metropolis, the river still has to

Above:
The Orival Rocks.

Facing page, top:
Louviers. A former monastery.

Facing page, bottom:
The church and vicinity.

pass through Elbeuf. Like Louviers, this town, which derives its name from the Viking Wellebou, also had clothmaking in its distant past, having been organized as a State manufacture by Colbert. Indeed textiles were woven here right up till the advent of modern industry. The stained-glass windows of the church of Saint-Etienne, like those of Notre-Dame de Louviers, are the sole witnesses to the age of the weavers, depicting those who were the life blood of Elbeuf taking part in their annual procession or at work in their normal attire.

The river then begins to wind its way past the base of the Orival Rocks, near the troglodyte village once inhabited by fullers, where the church of Saint-Georges can still be seen, partly hewn out of the cliff. From there it sets out on an enormous loop around Rouvray Forest and through Greater Rouen before swinging south almost to its point of departure, where

it flows through some very scenic and rugged terrain. As one would expect, the cliff which stands at this point, and provides a view quite as spectacular as that to be seen from Château-Gaillard, was once crowned by a castle – now half-ruined. According to legend it was built by Robert the Devil, a mythical figure who, in Brotonne Forest, is thought to have settled a dispute between an angel and a demon over the soul of a sinful monk. Actually this Robert was Robert the Magnificent, a descendant of Rollo and father of William, who in turn was given two sharply different nicknames: first, and much against his will, he was known as "the Bastard", before he later became William the Conqueror. Though largely destroyed in the 15th century to keep it out of English hands, this feudal castle nonetheless retains its proud bearing, with its crescent-shaped keep overlooking the valley. And this superb

vantage-point has another attraction, in its Viking museum: in the courtyard there is a lifesize reconstruction of a drakkar, or Viking boat, while a gallery of wax figurines, depicting the epic history of those who were to become the Normans, is laid out in the basement and the tower.

ROUEN: A MARITIME TRADITION

In 911, when Normandy was ceded to Rolf, also known as Rollo the Handsome, he decided to make Rouen the seat of this government.

Facing page:
View of the town surrounding the cathedral.

Below:
The bridges in Rouen.

The city already had a lengthy history, standing as it does on a highly privileged site – that of the first harbour inland from an estuary. Earlier still, the Gaulish tribe of the Veliocasses, after whom Le Vexin is named, had settled on the islets which provided easier access across the meandering river, and the Romans had founded Rotomagus, an active regional market and garrison town, on the same site. Saint Mellon began to evangelize the area in 260, and became the town's first bishop.

Fortunately, the Northmen were far better able than the Roman colonizers to produce a synthesis of two foreign cultures; in fact few conquerors have ever given so much to the conquered country. Having arrived in Rouen amidst the smoke of burning buildings, his sword dripping with blood, Rolf the Marcher converted to Christianity and became Robert I, Duke of Normandy, demonstrating a level of skills as an administrator which matched those he had once displayed at the head of his troops. This sea wolf can truly be regarded as the founder of the modern city, as the engineering projects he devised on the Seine were not completed until the 19th century. Far inland, but accessible to shipping on account of the tide, Rouen had embarked on a career making it the fourth largest port in today's France.

Its progress was not entirely smooth, however, and this prosperous city did occasionally fall on hard times. The transition to French control took place fairly gently, when Philippe-Auguste seized Rouen in 1204, and a first golden age followed, due to the success of the port and the clothmaking industries. The reconstruction of the cathedral and the abbey of Saint-Ouen date from this period. Then war returned, to join the epidemics of the plague and the famines which went on relentlessly. This Hundred Years' War began with a cruel siege, at the end of which the English seized control of the city in 1419. The resistance, inspired by the prowess of Joan of Arc, was crushed mercilessly; and the heroin herself, a victim of sordid intrigue, fell into the hands of the occupying forces. Then came the famous trial, after which the woman who was already a national symbol was burnt to death on the Place du Vieux-Marché. It was not until 1449 that Charles VII reconquered Rouen, which then experienced a Golden Century.

Rouen's succession of troubled and prosperous times was not over, however: first came the exodus of the industrious Protestant community due to the Revocation of the Edict of Nantes, and then the unexpected success of the woven and dyed cotton known as rouennerie. Fascination with this product proved beneficial to many branches of activity, and mechanization soon became widespread. The Normans, as enterprising as ever, also adopted the railroad and modernized their port, not with-

out inflicting some scratches in the process on their magnificent city. But this was nothing compared to the 1940 fire and the bombing at the end of the war; the damage came so close to complete annihilation that, half a century later, restoration work was still only barely complete.

However, as on previous occasions in Rouen's history, these tribulations brought with them some positive side effects. Industry disappeared from the left bank, being replaced by modern developments.

Top and left:
The Gros Horloge.

Facing page:
*The old houses
of the cathedral square.*

ROUEN: THE TRIUMPH
OF FLAMBOYANT GOTHIC

After Romanesque art, which had been carried to great heights by the Benedictines in their abbeys, the province returned to the French style, itself a development of Anglo-Norman, and arrived at an admirable synthesis between the pure proportions of antiquity and the decorative refinements of the new Gothic style.

The craft of the local masters triumphed, beginning in the 12th century, with Flamboyant Gothic, of which Rouen is indisputably the capital.

This light-filled Gothic, which derived from a notion of divinity less esoteric than was the case with the Romanesque period, and which was also nurtured by the prosperity of Rouen, was to reach higher and higher summits, and open out towards the heavens. In this way the

Cathedral of Notre-Dame de Rouen gradually evolved towards an ideal which it symbolizes today by its successful blending of lightness and majestic dimensions, overall harmony and extreme diversity.

Behind a dreary 19th century façade, Saint-Ouen is in fact one of the most complete specimens in France of the radiant Gothic style. This former abbey church, which, apart from its handsome soaring

Below:
Rouen. The entrance and spire of the cathedral.

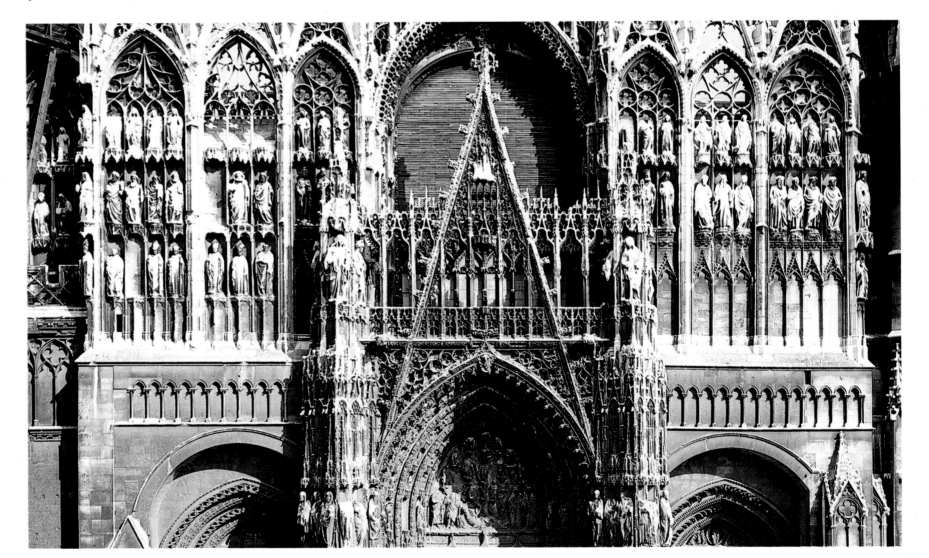

Above:
Rouen. The nave of the cathedral.

Right:
*The new belfry
of the St-Romain Tower.*

"crowned tower" looks quite ordinary from the outside, reveals its beauty once one has passed through the Marmousets Doorway. The concern for unity is evident in Saint-Maclou, just behind the cathedral, the distinctive feature of this church being the time it was built: though utterly Gothic in design, it was in fact constructed during the Renaissance. Here the virtuoso element is the façade, with its five arcades arranged in the shape of a fan, the pointed gables forming a kind of carved stone brazier at the foot of the lantern-tower.

Any account of the finest Gothic architecture of Rouen would be incomplete without the Law Courts, in which Corneille once practiced; this building is an exuberant example of late Gothic that already bears the imprint of the new ideas from Italy. However, the museum-city is in no sense confined to a profusion of medieval forms – as the people of Rouen themselves make abundantly clear by showing an equal fondness for the spire of Notre-Dame and also the famous Gros-Horloge, in a Renaissance setting.

Above and left:
The Law Courts at Rouen.

Facing page:
*A typical decorative detail
of the façade.*

THE HISTORY OF GREAT FIGURES IN ROUEN

The architectural splendors of Rouen have left its great men somewhat in the shade; indeed they were relegated to the background by a young woman from out of town who was briefly but spectacularly associated with its history.

The association between Joan of Arc and Rouen is not always presented in terms favorable to the city: yet it is a fact that its citizens never left the slightest doubt as to their fidelity to the French crown, paying in blood for their fierce resistance to English occupation. Even the treacherous Pierre Cauchon, self-appointed chief accuser, had come from Beauvais, where he was the local bishop. In fact the populace, harshly held in check by the troops of Lord Warwick, the local commander, who feared a revolt, caught sight of the saint only twice, when her judges forced her to recant on the scaffold of the cemetery of Saint-Ouen, and a few days later when she was put to death on the Place du Vieux-Marché. Charles VII, who had failed to render timely assistance to the woman without whom he would have lost all, at least had the decency to overturn the outcome of the trial and rehabilitate the heroin in the Grand Hall of the archbishop's palace, fifteen years after her death at the stake.

Until 1979, when the old covered market was partly replaced by one of

the most striking buildings in the whole city, the church of Saint Joan of Arc, built on the site of the church of Saint-Vincent which had been bombed during the Liberation, the name of the Place du Vieux-Marché had truly matched its function. This audacious piece of architecture, designed by Louis Arretche, is a direct continuation of the history of Rouen as it counterbalances the cathedral, situated at the far end of the Rue du Gros-Horloge, and also incorporates the spectacular stained-glass windows of the previous church, which were fortunately removed at the beginning of the war. The 65 ft. tall Cross of the Rehabilitation stands on the precise spot where the execution took place, and the Joan of Arc Museum is located in a fine traditional house on the square.

A few yards away, there is a small but interesting museum in the house where Pierre Corneille was born. The poet and playwright, the son of a Master of Forestry Commission, studied at the Jesuit College, a dignified building now named after him, where he trained for a legal career that was to lead to the post of prosecutor in the Parliament.

Facing page, left:
Rouen. The church of St-Maclou.

Facing page, right:
The central courtyard.

Above:
Detail of a façade.

Top:
Rouen. The church of St. Joan of Arc.

25

WRITERS AND ABBEYS

Literature, while rather cramped within the walls of Rouen, comes fully into its own on the higher ground of the outlying districts, from where there is such a fine view of the city.

The scene described by Maupassant is visible from Canteleu Hill, which can stand comparison with the famous Sainte-Catherine Hill; not far away, at Croisset, a Louis XV pavilion reverberates to the sound of Flaubert testing his manuscript by reading it out loud; at Petit Couronne we find the country house of the Corneille family, now a museum devoted to the playwright's memory; the Château of La Rivière-Bourdet, facing Roumare Forest, was for a time the setting for Voltaire's meditations on the banks of the Seine, but it is clearly the tragedy which befell the family of Victor Hugo that comes to mind when one thinks of that part of the river. Villequier, not far from where the poet's daughter drowned with her husband Charles while out sailing, is still graced by the splendid "brick house covered with green vines" of the Vacquerie family, the rich shipowners from Le Havre, whose sons vied with each other for the favor of Léopoldine. The building has now been turned into a Victor Hugo Museum, the third biggest in France, by virtue of its superb collections illustrating this somber period in Hugo's life, – the inspiration for series of poignant poems known as *The Contemplations.*

Above:
Ruins at Lillebonne.

Top:
View of Villequier.

Facing page, top:
*At La Haye-de-Routot,
the former bread oven.*

Facing page, bottom:
Lillebonne and its keep.

The dreaded tidal bore, now greatly subdued, caused another, though less famous shipwreck which still arouses the imagination of people living in the Lower Seine area – that of the Télémaque, that sank in 1790 just off Quillebeuf. The ship had left Rouen carrying the crown jewels, as well as the treasures of Boscherville and Jumièges abbeys: ever since, noone has succeeded in finding these priceless items Louis XVI was anxious to hide from the covetous grasp of the revolutionaries. The episode emphasizes yet again the importance of the abbeys of this historic valley, the heirs of those same congregations which had been such an easy prey for the Vikings on their way up the Seine. Once they had become converted, the conquerors and then their descendants made it a point of honor to rebuild the devastated communities with magnificent endowments; and they brought into being a Norman style some of the purest specimens of which, comparable to Caen or Mont-Saint-Michel, are to be found in the Lower Seine area.

Boscherville Abbey, at the edge of Roumare Forest, just outside Rouen, was founded in 1050 by Raoul de Tancarville, chamberlain to William the Conqueror; the present church was completed around 1125 by the Benedictines of Saint-Evroult, who eventually replaced the original cannons of the abbey. This building, which was saved from the pick-axe of the revolutionaries by the villagers of Saint-Martin, who preferred to sacrifice their own church and preserve the abbey church of Saint-Georges, is Upper Normandy's only unspoilt and unaltered structure from the heyday of the Norman Romanesque school. Its sober architecture, in which the imposing lantern-tower contrasts with the lightness of the façade, reveals to the observant visitor the beginnings of the Gothic period, in the pinnacle of the delicate staircase turrets.

The next loop in the river's course carries it around the majestic ruins of what was once the richest of French abbeys, in both temporal and spiritual terms, its influence reaching the very boundaries of Christianity for a thousand years. Jumièges can be traced back to the year 654, when St. Philibert founded, in a huge forest donated

by Clovis II, a monastery on which the Carolingian dynasty bestowed many favors. Such generosity unfortunately attracted the attention of the Vikings who, in three expeditions, eventually ruined Jumièges completely. By the time Duke William the long Sword, son of Rollo, discovered it by chance while out hunting, the community which had once formed a small town was reduced to two hermits living in shacks. The duke had the monastery restored and personally found for it a most distinguished abbot, William of Volpiano, from Lombardy. The new walls were inaugurated with the utmost solemnity by William the Conqueror, who had returned specially from his newly won domains the other side of the Channel. Jumièges was going not only to recover its past glory, but also to rise to even greater heights of brilliance in all spheres of thought and art, before

declining four centuries later with the start of the Hundred Years' War. It suffered a lengthy eclipse, but from 1666 onwards, the archbishops of Rouen succeeded in leading Jumièges into a third golden age, one whose splendours were cut short at the Revolution. As frequently happened in such cases, the buildings were used as barracks and then merely as stone-quarries. The architectural remains are nonetheless considerable, the two churches of Notre-Dame and Saint-Pierre being truly representative of a style that still bears the Carolingian imprint, while the early 12th century chapter house contains the oldest

known specimens of pointed arch vaulting.

The Abbey of Saint-Wandrille also lies within the Brotonne regional natural park, and is both one of the oldest and one of the youngest in the province. Wandrille, a former notable under King Dagobert, founded it in 649 on the banks of the Fontenelle, in a delightful setting which quickly came to be known as the Valley of the Saints, since they seemed to thrive there "like roses in a greenhouse". Though History has been less cruel to Saint-Wandrille than to Jumièges, nonetheless the Revolution left the abbey in ruins. The most noteworthy remains are those of the cloister, one of whose galleries dates from the early 14th century, while the three others are in the flamboyant style. The north gallery leads into the refectory, and includes a remarkable lavabo lavishly sculpted with Italianate motifs. After an assortment of hardships, the abbey returned to its original vocation in 1931, and once more echoes to the sound of Gregorian chant, on the initiative of Dom Pothier. The precious relics, which had been removed to Belgium for safe-keeping from the Vikings, have now been returned, eleven centuries later, and are housed in the new church, an early 13th century tithe barn which had been transported in pieces from La Neuville-du-Bosc, in the Eure.

Above:
Tancarville Bridge.

Facing page:
This great oak, christened "Cuve", has a circumference of almost 20 feet. It is one of the attractions of the forest of Brotonne.

Page 28 :
Jumièges: the remains of the abbey and detail of a sculpture.

Page 29 :
St Wandrille Abbey.

Above:
Brotonne bridge.

Above and left:
Views of Norman cottages.

Left:
Protective bread boxe.

A FERTILE AREA:
THE NORMAN VEXIN

"It's a deal!". Though never actually signed, the famous treaty of Saint-Clair-sur-Epte in fact amounted to nothing more than these words between Charles the Simple and Rolf the Marcher, accompanied by the gesture one associates with two horse-traders who have just clinched a deal.

With these golden words a modest river marking the boundary between the Norman and French Vexins was about to see its banks embellished with a number of châteaux, the most famous of these being Gisors, in the heart of a rolling gold and green landscape of large farms and forests rich with game. The ambitions of the Dukes of Normandy kept pace with their growing power over the centuries: in 1097 William the Redhead, son of the Conqueror, realized that the King of France might be able to take advantage of a weak spot along the Epte border. In order to replace the small seigniorial keep at Gisors, he brought in his engineer, Count Robert de Bellême, who advanced the art of fortification by building the first octagonal tower, joined to an elliptical chemise at the top of an

Above:
Dovecote at Mortemer Abbey.

Right, top and middle:
*Martainville Castle
and its kitchens.*

Right, bottom:
Vascœuil Castle.

artificial mound. As a result of this innovation the traditional square keep was made to look rather old fashioned. As the small town grew bigger, the dukes sought to enhance its defenses, by building outer fortified wall flanked by towers in 1125, and then adding two floors to the keep and buttresses to the chemise less than half a century later.

The French, who had already taken the fortress by treachery before being driven out, seized it again in 1193, taking advantage of the fact that Richard Lionheart was imprisoned in Austria. Philippe-Auguste then built a large circular keep, which is known today as the Prisoner's Tower as the dungeon beneath it is noted for the graffiti scratched on its walls by its occupants.

Along the Norman bank of the Epte Robert de Bellême also built the castle of Neaufles-Saint-Martin, visible from a long way off, its keep standing high on a mound; he was also doubtless closely involved in the design of the similar fortress, whose site is now occupied by a farm opposite Saint-Clair-sur-Epte. Castles at Dangu, Gaillard and Vernon completed the line of fortifications.

The Vexin plateaux are an area of fertile farmland, whose prosperity is made evident by the well built houses that can be seen dotted about them, frequently with an upper floor and a tile or slate roof occasionally covering a section of wall facing west. This latter feature occurs on the bell-

tower of the church at Lyons-la-Forêt – a town which is a worthy representative of the more heavily wooded part of the Norman Vexin, and is noted for its rather opulent architecture. The large beech forest which surrounds Lyons is one of the finest in France, thanks to the protracted stability it has enjoyed over the centuries, and which doubtless played a crucial part in its survival: in 1160 the monks from Mortimer served as veritable pioneers, in that they cleared the undergrowth, thus opening the area to lumberjacks, charcoal-burners and glassmakers, not to mention the powerful visitors who occasionally passed through, as the Lyons Forest was a royal hunting ground, and had been so since the time of the Merovingians. Any clearing that has been done in the forest has been strictly limited, and that is why Mortimer Abbey still enjoys, in Fouillbroc Valley, the truly Cistercian setting in which it was originally built. The Source Sainte-Catherine springs a short distance beyond the pond next to the abbey church and buildings. This spring is well known throughout Normandy, because there was a time when young women looking for a husband used to come to pray at the small oratory adjoining it.

Beyond the Andelle we enter the Bray region – quite a different landscape, where apple trees predominate, next to large cattle ranges. At Vascoeuil, near the confluence of the Crévon, the Château de la Forestière, with its handsome dovecote, has become a center for contemporary art, its grounds adorned with sculptures and mobiles. It was here that Michelet wrote part of his History of France. And that is not the only literary connection of the area. The nearby village of Ry provided Flaubert with his central inspiration for Madame Bovary. The local people had no trouble at all identifying the characters in the novel, which caused quite a stir at the time because it seemed obvious that the novelist had used as a model the wife of the local doctor.

Above:
The church of Saint-Denis at Lyons-la-Forêt, with its imposing church-tower wall, dates back to the 12th century. It contains polychrome wood statues from the 16th and 17th centuries.

Facing page and right:
Lyons-la-Forêt. Half-timbered façades and roofs.

FROM SPRINGS TO PASTURES: THE BRAY REGION

The Epte and the Andelle rise almost at the same point, near Forges-les-Eaux, while other more remote rivers – Thérain, Bresle and Béthune – also converge on this lush area.

The reason for this situation is a quirk of nature that geographers find particularly fascinating: the Bray region is a Perfect "buttonhole". In the tertiary period the regular strata in this part of the Paris basin were thrust upward, forming an elevated dome, from where the runoff flowed along all these rivers. Deep erosion then followed, causing the lower layers to become exposed one after the other. Their variety has produced the rather jumbled contours and diverse landscapes of the Bray region. Local detailed features make the reality a little more complex than this simplified outline would suggest. In fact a clear view of the buttonhole can be provided only by a geological map, where the appropriateness of its name becomes evident. Yet the landscape does bear traces of its existence: beneath the mud which accounted for the fertility of the southern Vexin, there emerges a silicate clay covered with forests, then a white or marly chalk containing the springs and, lastly, some plowed fields carpeting the valley, and the grasslands stretching over argillaceous soil.

This land, that had been neglected for a long time, was brought back to life by livestock farming, while the proximity of the capital permitted to sustain a dairy economy symbolized by the success of the "Petit Suisse". That same proximity was also good for tourism, because the warm water spa of Forges-les-Eaux owes its fame to Louis XIII, who went there to take the waters in 1633. His visit to the ancient city of blacksmiths could hardly have passed unnoticed, as the monarch was accompanied by Anne of Austria, Cardinal Richelieu and an armed escort several hundred men strong!

Facing page:
*At Beuvreuil, detail
of the church porch.*

Left:
*Remains of an 18th-century façade
at Forges-les-Eaux.*

Below:
Beeches in Eawy Forest.

The two poles of the Bray region are situated to the north and south of this spa town. Gournay-Ferrières, to the south, is a large cheese-making city surrounded by lush pastures. Its reputation can be traced back to the ingenuity of a local farmer's wife who sent her own cheeses to a businessman who had connections in Paris. One particular type, consisting of a blend of fresh and curdled cream, took the young man's fancy, so that he brought in Swiss experts and organized the industrial production of the cheese near Gournay.

Nonetheless a number of different landscapes go to make up this area, which also has its own splendid beech woodlands. Eawy Forest, which resembles Lyons Forest, and, like it, is associated both with the firing of artifacts such as the fine ceramics of Forges-les-Eaux, and with the royal hunt. The Château of Mesnières-en-Bray, one of the gems of the Norman Renaissance modeled after Chaumont, and formerly owned by Louis XV, for this reason has a long Stag Gallery in which the plaster statues carry real antlers.

Left and bottom:
*The Château of Eu and the crypt
in the chapel.*

Facing page:
View of Le Tréport.

THE OPAL COAST, EU AND LE TRÉPORT

Striking north from the Epte a string of ponds along the River Bresle marks the boundary between Normandy and Picardy, as decreed by the Treaty of Epte.

Two small towns at the mouth of the river have left their imprint on this Petit-Caux region: Le Tréport for the modern period and Eu for history, while Aumale, near the freshwater springs, seems content with its illustrious name. The Petit Caux is covered with the three forests of Eu once the property of the Dukes of Orleans. As usual both princes and peasants derived their various advantages from this arrangement. Lavish noble retinues would sweep through on the day's hunt, while around the forest's edge large numbers of glassmakers found good quality firewood for their ovens. When the efforts of Charles d'Artois culminated in the opening of a sea canal to the city of Eu, thus facilitating the delivery of coal, the manufacture of glass began to move into the lower part of the valley, where it is still to be found.

The city of Eu, so helpful in French crossword puzzles, derives its curious name from the Auga of Roman times, when it was the river port of the town of Augusta, which archeologists are now excavating a short distance away. After the establishment of the Norman state, Eu made its entry into History very much through the front door, as it witnessed the death of Rollo in 932, before becoming a county seat in 996. Its

location on the frontier was going to win it a far greater honour in 1050, on an occasion reported to us by the Bayeux Tapestry: the wedding of William the Conqueror and his cousin, Mathilde of Flanders. The bride needed some persuading, as William was still William the Bastard and had only just secured his title to the duchy; yet she eventually gave her consent. The ceremony, which took place at the border between the spouses respective domains, was a grand affair, as the Queen Mathilde Tapestry shows. In fact this work of art is all that we know about the original Eu Castle, Louis XI had destroyed in 1475 in order to prevent the King of England from taking advantage of it. There was clearly still a long way to go before the Entente Cordiale…

A hundred years later, Scarface, otherwise known as the Duke of Guise, commissioned an architect from Beauvais to build the brick and stone residence which we admire today. After his murder, his widow, who had owned the estate at the time of their marriage, retired there; their mortal remains lie in the magnificent marble mausoleums in the College Chapel. Delighted that she could see the sea from her apartments, Louis XIV's cousin, the Grande Demoiselle, then acquired the château, built the wings and had Le Nôtre renovate the grounds.

There are few openings in the cliffs along the Opal Coast, so that the mouth of the Bresle was used, at an early stage in its history as a port. Until the beginning of the 19th century, when the wharves and jetties commissioned by Bonaparte were built and later on, when high society came, in response to the regal fashion set by Louis-Philippe, Le Tréport was not a particularly noteworthy place. The proximity of Paris, the picturesque fishing harbour, the beaches and the cliffs all did the rest, and it is now a popular seaside resort.

DIEPPE
AND SEA-BATHING

All the assets which ensured the success of Le Tréport on the Opal Coast are also to be found at Dieppe, which was favoured as much by nature as by events.

The great city which shares a prominent role on the Alabaster Coast with Fécamp is in fact situated at the mouth of the Arques, a short river formed by the merging of the Béthune and its two main tributaries, that is powerful enough to have carved its own estuary through the rampart of the towering Caux cliffs. Moreover the bed of the Arques is remarkably deep – so much so that it gave its name to the city, "Dieppe" being a Norman corruption of the English "deep". Quite early in the history of the province this ability to receive deep-sea ves-

Above:
Dieppe. The castle.

Top:
Dieppe. The cliffs.

Facing page:
Dieppe. The port.

sels made Dieppe a port capable of handling shipping to remote destinations. It was thus to Normandy what Saint-Malo was not yet to Brittany – its daring sailors, explorers and corsairs being supported by enterprising merchants and shipowners. Such good fortune, however, had the undesirable effect of attracting covetous ambitions: each resulting conflict brought with it a new share of destruction. Lastly, since its beach is closer than any other to Paris and it had one of the first rail lines, Dieppe can boast of being the dean – a rather young dean, however – of the seaside resorts of France. Indeed it actually inaugurated the era of seaside bathing.

Its wharves, with names like Tonkin, India or Morocco, a dock called the Bassin du Canada, the old town, Le Pollet where fresh fish and scallops have for centuries been landed, on their way to the fine tables of Paris, with bulk carriers and the Newhaven car-ferries – all this means that, despite its great age, Dieppe has not lapsed into monotony or sluggishness. Here one is treated to an ever-changing spectacle.

In this city flattened by heavy fighting during the last war, in particular the attempted landing of Canadian troops in August 1942, visitors eager to see interesting architecture must be content with the church of Saint-Jacques. Since its construction that started in 1250, this building has been steadily altered, right up to the present day, some of its stonework surviving each conflict. Of special interest is the Treasury, contained within a wall richly sculpted in the 16th century with exotic motifs from the five continents.

The castle towering over the town from a terrace on the cliff, has a greater unity of style, as most of it was built in the 15th century. Inside the interesting local museum it contains, there is not only an exhibit devoted to the great seafarers of Dieppe, of whom the most famous is Duquesne, but also a room in honour of Camille Saint-Saëns, who was a Dieppois at heart. Yet the most remarkable collections are those of carved ivory, in which the city has specialized since 1365, and the paintings that accompanied the emergence of Dieppe as a seaside resort. Bathing in the sea was made fashionable by Queen Hortense, who used to spend her summers in Dieppe, sometimes in the company of the official court painter, Jean-Baptiste Isabey, Eugène Isabey's Father; the latter, in a less academic style, painted the portrait, "facing the unleashed forces of nature", of Duchess Marie-Caroline de Berry, another celebrity who helped put the resort on the map by bathing in the sea, lavishly dressed, and arm in arm with the deputy prefect. For its part, the painting attracted numerous artists, such as Boudin, Renoir, Degas and Gauguin to the region, where they stayed, being delighted with its delicate shades of light. Musicians and writers were likewise swayed by the charms of the area. And from the other side of the Channel came

Turner, Bonington and others, years ahead of the modern British tourist.

Some big names in the art world have taken a liking to Varengeville, not far from Dieppe; these include Georges Braque, who had a studio there, and also Albert Roussel, both of whom lie buried in its small, isolated cemetery. But the enchantment of the area dates back much further than that, because in 1530 the most powerful shipowner of the day also chose Varengeville as the site of his country residence; the Ango manor is a sumptuous Florentine villa transposed to a Norman setting. It was worthy of the visit made to it by François I, the royal friend of the viscount of Dieppe. However, the manor does not owe its present fame to that visit, but to an extraordinary dovecote with a polychrome facing made of brick, flint and sandstone, beneath a striking bulbous domed roof.

Facing page:
Ango Manor.

Below:
The coast, at Varengeville. The region's subtle harmonies of colour have attracted many painters, the Impressionists included.

THE CAUX REGION AND THE ALABASTER CLIFFS

Those who have not yet had a chance to discover its discreet charms are quite likely to find the landscape of the Caux region, with its fairly straight roads, rather tame. The English Channel, moreover, is often grey and not particularly romantic.

Even so, the point at which these two wholly different landscapes come abruptly face to face tends to overshadow the rest of the Caux region, so that for most visitors it tends to be synonymous with the cliffs of the Alabaster Coast. This majestic coastline, open to the sea breezes and pounded by the waves, was also "discovered" in the middle of the last century by artists seeking their inspiration in nature. Whether they were inclined towards romanticism, like Delacroix or Courbet, sought vibrant nuances, like Corot, Monet or Pissaro or had elaborated a more contrived style, like Signac or Matisse, the shores of the Caux region always met their aspirations by veiling the wild beauty of the cliffs in a sky of gauze.

This remarkably steep slope, which exposes a dazzling white mass of chalk, striped with dark lines of flint, is an open wound in the continent gnawn, nibbled or devoured by the sea, depending on the spot. At Cape

Above:
The cliffs at St-Valery-en-Caux.

Left:
The famous oak at Allouville-Bellefosse.

La Hève the cliff occasionally retreats over six feet in a single year, eroded by the rain, cracked open by the frost, and undermined at the base, where all that remains is an expanse of flint pebbles, formed from the disintegration of rock strata, across which the sea surges noisily. In fact the coastline is receding everywhere, as can be seen in the ruins of a huge Gallo-Roman oppidum right on the shore itself near Veulettes. It is easy to see how the legend of a sunken city could have come into being in such a place. As a result of this natural phenomenon a large number of streams, which did not flow strongly enough to be able to steer a new course and cut their way through to the sea, found themselves high and dry. These are the valleuses, – the hanging valleys formed when runoff simply drained into cracks in the underlying rock – so characteristic of the Alabaster

Coast. Certain other valleys which though dry are also quite lush, come close enough to the coast to provide a haven for fishing villages or small seaside resorts; but Dieppe, Saint-Valéry-en-Caux and Fécamp, situated at the mouths of major indentations, are exceptions in this landscape, as can be seen from the volume of shipping passing through their harbours.

The hinterland, far from being nondescript, contains features which deserve some attention from the visitor. We should at least dwell a moment on the highly distinctive masures (farmhouses) scattered about between the pastures and the fields of flax. This unique type of abode was the response of the inhabitants of the Caux region to the strong winds which assaulted them after the destruction of the forests. The farm buildings occupy a quadrangle surrounded by an embankment where

oaks, beech or elms grow; the roofs are often thatched, with irises planted at the top, in keeping with an ancient Celtic tradition. This delightful farmhouse cumcourtyard is likely to remain the symbol of the Caux region.

The main market town in this area is also something of a symbol, having been made famous in a song by Béranger (The King of Yvetot), thanks to a quirk of history. There really was a King of Yvetot in the 15th and 16th centuries, by virtue of one of the fanciful arrangements which tended to occur about that time; in fact he had judicial powers over all matters, both great and small, and issued leather currency. A few miles from Yvetot we come to one of the oldest trees in France, the thousand-year-old oak at Allouville-Bellefosse, which is the center of a pilgrimage. One should not, therefore, be surprised to find that its huge trunk houses two chapels, one above the other! Other more modest archi-

Above:
The cliffs of Fécamp.

Left, top:
Fécamp. Inside the Benedictine Museum.

Left, bottom:
The town of Fécamp.

tectural specimens are, of course, scattered about the extensive Caux Plateau, which has always been swept by the winds of history. These include, for example, the feudal ruins of Arques-la-Bataille, which bring to mind the desperate but victorious struggle of the future Henry IV, who was besieged here by the Catholics, or the Renaissance walls of Miromesnil, within which Guy de Maupassant, the most celebrated storyteller of the Caux region, was born.

However, Fécamp, the town where the writer lived, is where the region's architectural gems are situated hemmed in at the mouth of the Valmont, between the tallest cliffs of the coast. The legend surrounding the relic of the Precious Blood made Fécamp the major shrine in Normandy, long before Mont-Saint-Michel. The wealth of the original abbey attracted the predatory atten-

tion of the Vikings; yet Rollo's successors, once they had settled at Fécamp, restored its magnificence and its influence a hundredfold. They built the abbey church of the Trinity and a monastery, appointing as its abbot the great Guillaume de Volpiano, from Cluny. Because of its cathedral like dimensions, and to an even greater extent because of its style and the artworks it contains, this church is one of the principal architectural attractions of the province, and is still venerated by numerous pilgrims. The Benedictines of this monastery, formerly called the Gate to Heaven, also set in motion another pilgrimage, this time of a wholly secular nature. In 1510 a monk specializing in the art of herbal remedies, invented an elixir of health, whose recipe disappeared during the Revolution but was rediscovered by a certain Alexander Legrand. The liqueur known as Benedictine

had begun its triumphant career. The museum devoted to it is located in a striking monastic palace built in the late 19th century by a follower of Viollet-Le-Duc, whose grasp of specific styles was not always too sound. The buildings themselves are, however, most interesting as they provide a fine setting for some superb art collections, together with all that could be salvaged from the old abbey.

ETRETAT, A CHALK THEATRE

Etretat and its cliffs should be credited with popularizing this section of the coast so well that they, like Raz Point, have become merged with the collective subconscious mind.

To start with, the faithful were painters and writers; in 1823 Isabey, who also "discovered" Trouville, began to visit Etretat to paint seascapes and still-lifes with fish, while Alphonse Karr depicted the local scene enthusiastically in his novels, adding: "If a friend was about to see the sea for the first time, I would take him to Etretat". Film, rather than canvas, is now the medium of choice for recording its scenic beauties; however, its appeal is still as great as ever, judging by the number of summer visitors who come to this pretty pink-hued resort, nestling inside its lush valley.

At one time there remained few traces of the community of fishermen who toiled at Le Perrey, under the studious gaze of Courbet or Monet, so the decision was taken to restore some of the caloges of the old tidal dock at Etretat. These old boats, with their tired frames, were converted into sheds for fishing gear, having been first tarred and then given a thatch roof. Beyond this fisherman's beach, which has recovered its local colour, stands the Aval Cliff, with its famous Gate, in which Maupassant saw "an elephant plunging his trunk into the sea". As for the equally famous Needle (Aiguille), more than 200 ft. tall, facelorg it, Maurice Leblanc was prompted by it to write one of his most successful novels, The Hollow Needle, in which the illustrious gentleman-burglar Arsène Lupin, had concealed his hideaway inside this limestone obelisk. Next along the cliffs we come to the valleuse of Jambour, within which the Petit-Port is located, and the Man-

neporte, a massive archway through which it is possible to walk at low tide. Further seaward, from the Custom Agents' Trail (Sentier des Douaniers) it is possible to see, inside another needle, the Damsels' Chamber (Grotte des Demoiselles) – a legendary cave described in detail by Maupassant. This world of cliffs and pebbles, wedged between sea and countryside, was in fact the playground of the author's childhood; later on, after he had become successful, he often returned to La Guilette, the house he had built at Etretat. Now it seems like just another chalet, among the more recent vacation homes which lie nestled in the hollow of the valley and which really make up the flesh of a city whose historic core consists only of the covered market and the church of Notre-Dame. Apart from the lantern-tower, dating from the early Gothic period, this church, originally subordinate to Fécamp Abbey, is an interesting specimen of the Norman Romanesque style.

Standing like a lookout at the edge of the Amont Cliff, the squat shape of Notre-Dame-de-la-Garde rather reminds one of some Breton chapel, with its distinctive walls.

Left and above:
Assorted views of Etretat.

Facing page:
Etretat. The covered market.

Following pages:
The famous cliffs of Etretat make a highly dramatic landscape. At its highest point the sheer, sea-eroded cliff face drops some 250 feet down to the sea below.

51

AN OCEANIC VOCATION: LE HAVRE

The name Le Havre has come to be associated with nostalgic and fading images of the departure on transatlantic voyages of the great liners of the past.

Such as the grandest, most lavish vessel of all, the almost mythical Normandie, even though the war and the growth of air travel have eliminated all memories of that period from the city itself. Located at the top of the Caux region and the mouth of the Seine Valley, Le Havre could hardly have failed to be the Gateway to the Ocean – a title which is strongly expressed in architectural terms by the monumental perspective of Avenue Foch.

Like Saint-Nazaire, only at an earlier age, the port of Le Havre was entirely man-made, having been built among the marshes of the mouth of the river in order to offset the silting up of Honfleur, Leu, Caudebec and Harfleur, further upstream. The decision was made in 1517 by François I, and the chapel of Notre-Dame-de-Grâce, the solitary house of worship in these marshlands, gave its name, Hâvre (Haven) de Grâce, to the new port, designed by Jérôme Bellarmato in the Venetian style. At the end of the war, when Le Havre, the most heavily damaged city in France, was simply a pile of ruins, many people were shocked to see the task of reconstruction entrusted to Auguste Perret, in whose eyes concrete was a wholly self-sufficient and noble building material. Yet one wonders whether it would have been possible at all to rebuild the old Le Havre, and indeed whether history had truly left much of

an imprint on the old city. The new city blocks, with their low clean lines, extend around the Boulevard François I, from the Rue de Paris to the arcades which bring to mind those of Rivoli, and from the Avenue Foch (the local version of the Champs-Elysées) and the Place de l'Hôtel de Ville all the way to the Porte Océane. In keeping with the rythm of Perret's original plan, these buildings allowed for plenty of light and flowery spaces, and do not detract from the prominence of the city's two landmarks: the Hôtel de Ville and the church of Saint-Joseph.

In this port complex, whose gigantic scale is symbolized by the François I dock, which is unmatched anywhere in the world, the huge piles of containers and the industrial road runing along the estuary, have somewhat destroyed the picturesque charm of the landscape. However, a boat ride through

the glistening waters of the harbour reveals a fascinating world, of gentle but powerful monsters, which has an inherent artistic appeal all of its own. Boats leave from the marina beyond which, behind the north breakwater, stretches the very popular beach of Le Havre; thereafter, the coast rises again, with the cliffs of Sainte-Adresse and Cape La Hève.

The high ground which rings the city to the north provides many vantage points looking down over the port and the lower part of the city.

Top:
Le Havre. The yacht harbour.

Facing page:
The church of Notre-Dame.

Right: *The Normandy bridge, spanning the Seine estuary at Le Havre, is the largest suspension bridge in the world.*

HONFLEUR: A FASCINATING CITY
FOR PAINTERS

When Raoul Dufy exclaimed: "I pity any painter who was not born on the banks of a river or by the sea!" he must surely have had in mind Eugène Boudin, a son of Honfleur and inspired self-taught man whose eye, as befits a seafarer, could decipher the mirages of sun, water and sky in this restless Seine Bay.

Could there be a better place for such gifts to come to maturity than this town, with its delicate charm, bathed in such a unique light? Painters who have known Honfleur have all tried to tame its reflections on canvas, just as Boudin once admitted that he "caressed a cloud like a woman's shoulder". With his friends Jongkind, Courbet, Monet and even Baudelaire who wrote his Invitation to travel while in Honfleur, this precursor made his home town the cradle of a new school of painting. For the past century and a half, artists have been retracing the steps of these visionaries, seeking that special light tinged with the grey of silver, slate or lead, that fluid, vibrant yet perennial moment along the streets and the waterfront or on the hill at Honfleur. Many others come to Honfleur in order to enjoy the simple harmony of a unique port which is very much alive, though in a setting straight from the past, and authentic in every detail. Honfleur, which is neither a fossilized museum-town, behind artificial façades, nor rows of souvenir shops, truly deserves its title of Pearl of the Estuary.

This port, behind which lies the wooded plateau of the Côte de Grâce, came into being about the same time as the duchy itself. As a result of a number of English raids, what was initially a fishing village soon found itself fortified. Once peace had been restored at the beginning of the 16th century, its mariners busied themselves with commerce and long-distance expeditions; moreover, they were occasionally not above a little piracy. New ports of call in Brazil, Labrador, Newfoundland and Sumatra were promptly turned into profitable fishing destinations, trading posts and even colonies – as was the case with Quebec, which was founded in 1608 by Champlain and his crews from Honfleur. In order to

Left:
Honfleur. The Old Harbour.

Facing page:
Houses along the waterfront.

Following pages:
Honfleur. Overall view.

56

expand the amount of berthing space available to the port the fortifications were demolished in 1690, and huge salt warehouses were built to supply the cod boats. At this point the sailors and shipowners of Honfleur enjoyed a golden age, with no fear of competition from Le Havre. This prosperity came to an end with the loss of the New World territories; during the 18th century the port settled into relative oblivion, handling nothing bigger than coastal vessels and local fishing boats. The economy then revived to some extent with the lumber trade, though not enough to make the town strategically important; accordingly it emerged from the Second World War unscathed. Its new facilities, located

slightly out of town, have now made Honfleur a dynamic port.

The older part of Honfleur immediately surrounds the Old Dock (Vieux Bassin), which was dug on the initiative of Duquesne, and later extended as far as the site of the moats, after the demolition of the ramparts. The events of this period account for the rather unusual appearance of the houses bordering the quays, as the land thus made available against the counterscarp was divided into narrow plots – a fact which compelled the builders to pile the rooms up on top of each other, sometimes reaching a total of six or seven stories. The extreme diversity of the building materials and methods used

Above:
Honfleur. The church of Notre-Dame-de-Grâce.

Facing page, top:
Honfleur. The Caen Gate.

Facing page, bottom:
Honfleur. La Lieutenance.

combined to make the Old Dock area look like something out of a fairytale. La Lieutenance, or Governor's House, precisely the kind of castle one would expect to find in such a story, is located near the swing bridge; it is in fact the former Caen Gate, sole surviving part of the ramparts, just opposite the chestnut-wood belltower of the church of Saint-Etienne, now a navy museum. In the church of Sainte-Catherine the people of Honfleur, who generated a considerable amount of unusual architecture, built themselves a truly unprecedented place of worship. Stonecarvers were in short supply after the Hundred Years' War, so they managed with whatever resources they could find; today, as one looks at the double nave, entirely made of wood and strikingly resembles a pair of upturned hulls, one can easily imagine scores of naval carpenters busily applying their skills to a vessel which would never leave port. And for them nothing could have been simpler than the belltower, built in the middle of the triangular marketplace, right over the bell-ringer's house; it is well supported on oak crutches, and is covered with slates and shingles, in keeping with local tradition.

From the opulent mansions of the Rue Haute, much favoured by shipowners, to the cart-tracks which had been laid out to fit the size of contemporary axles, towards the woods of the Côte de Grâce, Honfleur has other charms in store which, though less spectacular, are just as appealing. These are the art galleries and antique shops of the Enclos, the exhibitions of modern art, beneath the historic beams of the salt warehouses, and also various craftsmen, still using ancestral methods to work a forge, a binding press or a glass oven.

VERNIER MARSH AND THE
NORMAN CORNICHE

The Normandy of wet glistening grasslands described by Lucie Delarue-Mardrus, a poet from Honfleur, starts at the famous Saint-Siméon Inn; the sight of the open woodlands known as bocage has fascinated painters almost as much as the sky and the water.

Bazille, who often set up his easel next to Monet's, used to say: "This place is sheer paradise. Nowhere else can one find more beautiful trees or lush grass. The sea, or rather a greatly broadened Seine forms a delightful horizon for these waves of green..." The nearby hill known as the Côte de Grâce was the subject of an admirable painting by Corot; it is a popular place for a stroll high above Honfleur, and from near there the Calvary provides a sweeping view of the bay. A short distance away, the chapel of Notre-Dame-de-Grâce, surrounded by magnificent trees, is a major shrine built by the local people in around 1600 to replace the earlier structure built for the pilgrimage in the early years of the duchy by Robert the Magnificent.

The appeal of the landscape along the outer edge of the Auge region, which has remained unchanged since the time of the Impressionists, is due largely to its great diversity. Towards the two queens of the seaside, Trouville and Deauville, the Norman Corniche, passes by some splendid vacation homes and three picturesque villages: Vasouy, which is connected to the sea by a stairway; Cricqueboeuf, whose church, a rustic ivy-covered chapel from the 12th century, is reflected in a pond; and Villerville, which welcomes both fishermen and holidaymakers in its rocky inlet. The Saint-Gatien Forest, before the Touques Valley, marks the southernmost limit of the Lieuvin Plateau, which is bounded in the opposite direction by the Risle and land now covered with orchards growing where the Seine once wound its way to the sea. With hedges sometimes taller than a coppice, clusters of appel trees, lush grasslands dotted here and there with piebald cows and deep valleys cutting across the open woodlands, this is a quintessentially Norman landscape.

Our surprise is all the greater, therefore, when we come to the lowlands stretching beyond the Risle, with the Vernier Marsh set in a crown of hills. Here the horses have nothing in common with the thoroughbreds of the Côte Fleurie, since they are the wild brothers of the Camargue horse with white mane and tail; even the cows seem to be from a bygone age, with their thick hair, from which their horns protrude menacingly. The Brotonne Regional Natural Park has included Vernier Marsh within its confines; and, while one should avoid comparing it too closely with the Camargue, there is nonetheless an intense pleasure to be derived from a leisurely and quiet walk about this protected area.

Above:
The famous Saint-Siméon Manor.

Right:
*The ivy-covered chapel at
Criquebœuf.*

Facing page:
Aerial view of the port of Honfleur.

LITERATURE IN THE OUCHE REGION

Tradition has it that the Risle marks the boundary between Upper and Lower Normandy, but these rather academic terms fail to convey the easily perceptible realities of the landscape.

The lower stretch of the river flows between distinct areas such as Roumois, Neubourg and Lieuvin; whereas further upstream with the Charentonne it slices in two the cold expanses of the Ouche region. The originality of this part of Normandy does not lie only in its landscapes but also in its colourful people; characters and situations drawn from this extensive reservoir occur in the works of a number of writers – such as La Varende's petty squires noisily upholding their honour, the irresistible and extravagant passions of the heroes of Barbey d'Aurevilly, or the juicy scenes from everyday life described with such relish by the Comtesse de Ségur.

L'Aigle, at the end of the Normandy Perche, is a town which combines some of these peculiarities: its houses, with their tiled roofs, are made of flint or ocher and pink bricks, while the church of Saint-Martin adds yet another special feature – a curious local stone called grison that looks like gingerbread. This is an agglomerate with a high iron content which, in the early part of the 19th century, brought about an economic recovery in a region that had previously been limited to low-yield agriculture. At that time all the mills in the upper Risle Valley were turned into foundries and metalworking shops producing needles and staples; the modern factories which today power the local economy derived from these modest beginnings. Nouettes Castle, which is located near from a group of these factories at Aube-sur-Risle, is now a children's home, though it was once where the Comtesse de Ségur, author of Model Young Girls used to live. The nearby Ségur-Rostopchine Museum recreates the atmosphere in which this simple yet sophisticated woman of the world used to live. The metal-working tradition lives on at Rugles, a few miles downstream, whereas La Ferrière's connection with iron, which doubtless went back to ancient times, now lies solely in its name.

Before following the river any further a slight diversion will take us to one of the historically important

places in this region, Conches-en-Ouche, a city with a tumultuous past – as one might guess from its location, perched on a rocky spur at a bend in the Rouloir. In Old French, conche means "shell", which is also the etymology of another town, Conques de Rouergue, as both of them trace their origins back to a sanctuary dedicated to Sainte Foy, containing her relics. The present building, whose spire is not in particularly good condition, dates from the end of the 15th century and has one of the finest sets of Renaissance stained-glass windows in the province.

Large forests cover this part of the Ouche region as far as the Risle and Beaumont-le-Roger, where hunting in the grand style still takes place. The most interesting feature of this former domain of the Dukes of Normandy, over which some fierce fighting took place, particularly between Richard Lionheart and Philippe-Auguste, is

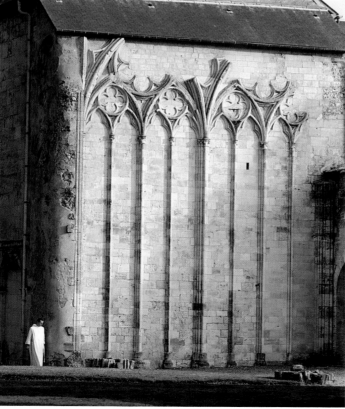

Above:
Bec-Hellouin Abbey: the cloister and the monastery buildings.

Left:
Bec-Hellouin Abbey: remains of the abbey church.

Facing page:
Bec-Hellouin Abbey: the St-Nicolas-Tower.

the church of Saint-Nicolas, with its mixture of 15th century and modern stained glass.

The river is then swollen by the waters of the Charentonne, a fine and secluded setting for fishing which also flows through Bernay, the chief town in these parts, grown around the first Romanesque abbey in Normandy. Founded by Guillaume de Volpiano at the request of Judith of Brittany, wife of Duke Richard II, it has now recovered its original quiet magnificence, after the completion of painstaking restoration work. The second ranking town in the Charentonne, the much smaller Broglie, used to be called Chambrais; it was given its present name in the 18th century when the Broglie family, from Piedmont, built the château which looks down over it. This residence, with its three hundred windows, contains a most extraordinary library which was patiently assembled by three marshals, two presidents of the council and one Nobel price winner. It is

nicely matched by the quintessentially Baroque Château of Beaumesnil, a few miles away, with its museum of bookbinding, which includes the collections of the National Library and the Furstenburg Foundation.

At the confluence of the Risle and the Charentonne Le Bec-Hellouin Abbey is the dominant presence in the area, because Brionne, a historic city which has one of the few square keeps in Normandy, was also the home of the 11th century knight Herluin. Moved by divine grace he founded in a slightly lower valley the monastery which was to wield such a powerful influence over the Western world for six centuries. After this pioneer the Italian Lanfranc gave the abbey a continental dimension by going to Rome to persuade the pope to rescind his ban on the marriage of Duke William to his cousin Mathilde of Flanders. As a result he was made Archbishop of Canterbury; his compatriot Anselme, before succeeding him in that post, succeeded in turning

Above:
West façade of the Château of Beaumesnil.

Facing page, top:
A farm at Bernay.

Facing page, bottom:
The dovecote and the outbuildings of the Château of Launay.

Le Bec-Hellouin into a spiritual beacon. The belltower of Saint-Nicolas, which stands apart from the abbey church, has been preserved; from its balustrade adorned with pinnacles one can see the valley and the harmonious layout of this retreat, with the monastery buildings situated at a right angle to the Cour de France and the Italianate cloister.

There was a time when the branches of the Risle near the mouth of the river were navigable, and a prosperous town, a kind of "Norman Venice", grew up around the spot where the first bridge was built over the river. This town, where tanning has long been an important industry, still has some fine timbered houses such as those in the Cour de Canel, and the church of Saint-Ouen, whose superb early stained glass windows illustrate the legend of its patron saint.

TROUVILLE AND THE FAMOUS BOARDWALK OF DEAUVILLE

The sight of these two middle-aged sisters, with their feet in the sand, one of them prim and proper while the other prances about skittishly before its very eyes, readily suggests the kind of relationship which must exist between them.

In fact there is much more than the width of the Touques dividing Trouville from Deauville, the two rivals of the Côte Fleurie. Their history is certainly worth considering.

In this final bend of the Touques, everything started at Trouville, a plain fishing village transfigured by the fresh gaze of Romanticism. From the beginning of the 19th century painters and writers were attracted to this picturesque haven, first living with local inhabitants and later at Mme Oseraie's inn. In 1836, when the adolescent Flaubert made the acquaintance of Mme Schlesinger, the great love of his life who inspired his precocious Memoirs of a Madman, it was already in the distinguished setting of the Agneau d'Or inn; a few years later, at the beginning of the Second Empire, this regular patron found it deplorable that "Paris has invaded this poor place, now full of chalets in the style of those at Enghien." Trouville's worldly success was however only in its early stages: these vacation homes, whose style was more often Swiss than Norman, were particularly concentrated on the slopes of Aguesseau Hill, above the fishing harbour. Later on high society invaded the beach area, where an initial casino, located under a marquee, was quickly replaced by an unduly elaborate oriental structure, which in turn was succeeded by the enormous white building, in the style of Louis XVI and is now surrounded by big hotels. From then on, people vied with one another to see who could build the most unusual or the most luxurious villa along the sea front, in

Above:
The harbour at Trouville.

Facing page, top:
The beach at Trouville.

Facing page, bottom:
Trouville. Overlooking the sea.

a frenzied display of kitsch, the results of which are still visible on the corniche.

Trouville was running out of space. Towards 1860 a stretch of marshland on the far shore, at the foot of Mount Canisy, where the small village of Deauville lay dormant, attracted the attention of a group of speculators. They included, in particular, the Duke of Morny, the banker Lafitte, Prince Davidoff and Dr. Oliffe: their villas, some of which launched the "Norman rustic" style, set off a spectacular building boom on the other bank of the Touques. It also happened that the railroad terminal was established on that side; a dock was built, and the Hippodrome, which was going to do

as much for the success of Deauville as the famous Boardwalk, was inaugurated in 1900. The social supremacy of the new resort ceased to be in any doubt when the mayor of Trouville, having lost the 1911 election, himself crossed the Pont des Belges, in order to found a casino and the sumptuous Hotel Normandy in Deauville, thus venting his feelings on the thankless rival resort which he had helped launch.

It seems that nothing can suppress the dynamism of Deauville, whose post-war growth – a second race course, a pool and a salt-water spa – is dwarfed by the size and magnificence of Port-Deauville, a marina built on land reclaimed from the sea,

incidentally blocking part of the horizon as seen from Trouville. Deauville still attracts a cosmopolitan, refined clientèle; its atmosphere, while at times disconcerting, is quite inimitable. The Grand Prix, followed by the famous ball, the gala horse races leading to the award of the Cravache d'Or (Golden Whip), the polo matches, the regattas organized by the Yacht Club, the fashion parades and the high society dinners, where anyone who is anyone tries to be seen.

Though it has been left far behind in the high society sweepstakes, Trouville has nonetheless retained a reputation of its own; in fact it has made good use of the qualities that distinguish it from Deauville by cultivating a slightly dating charm. Coastal fisheries are still an important business, operating from the heart of the town. Trouville also has its boardwalk, which runs past an ecological aquarium containing thousands of species, a modern saltwater spa and a most interesting museum of painting. It is situated in the Villa Montebello, whose ornate 1870 façade stands out above its neighbours on the seafront. Its collections show the extent to which the birth of the resort was associated to the artists of the early 19th century: Eugène Isabey, Charles Mozin whom many people regard as the true "discoverer" of Trouville, Eugène Boudin and Honoré Daumier, whose irreverent drawings show us an amusing picture of seaside bathing, at a time when ladies were taken to the water's edge in harnessed cabins. Raoul Dufy, Van Dongen and André Rambourg came later.

Left:
The race course of La Touques (the enclosure).

Below:
Deauville: the Boardwalk.

Facing page:
Deauville: the casino.

TASTY FOOD IN THE AUGE REGION

The hinterland of the Côte Fleurie, around the Touques Valley and as far as the Côte d'Auge, just before the River Dives, is a concentrated expression of all the lushness of Normandy.

The undulating relief of the landscape is buried beneath superb woodlands growing on a soil consisting of clay mixed with flint and generally thought to be rather infertile. One has to go behind this "dish of raw wicker", which Flaubert found so distasteful, to find Normandy's land of milk and honey. The apple trees blossoms, dotted about the fields like so many bridal bouquets, means cider and calvados; the plump bulls provide meat for demanding Parisian palates; the cows, speckled brown or black, are cream and butter; the half-timbered farmhouses, with thatched or slate roofs, are attached to dairies making famous cheeses such as Livarot, Pont-l'Evêque or Camembert; while the poultry clucking between the outhouses bring to mind the tasty dish known as Poulet vallée d'Auge, served with scallions. Besides this kind of livestock farming, which supplies gourmet tables, there is another, practised in the aristocratic environment of the manors dotted about the Auge region – the small studfarms which vie with each other to produce thoroughbred horses.

In this setting of plenty and good taste, a picturesque town, Pont-l'Evêque, has risen to fame since the Middle Ages, when it was described in the Roman de la Rose (1230) by Guillaume de Lorris, as "tender and smooth". This could only have hap-

Facing page, top:
An old façade at Pont-l'Evêque.

Facing page, bottom:
The church of St-Germain-de-Livet.

Below:
The castle of St-Germain-de-Livet.

Right:
*Fortified gateway
to Fervaques Castle.*

pened in the Auge region, as fresh creamy milk, still warm, is a necessity. The town after which the cheese is named is located in the middle of a plain of grasslands where the Calonne and the Yvie converge towards the Touques; at this well-endowed spot one of the first bishops of Lisieux built a bridge. Like Pont-Audemer, this crossing over the river, which all traffic was obliged to use, had become a regional market by the year 1000, and then the seat of local government – a status which it lost to Lisieux only in modern times. Therefore, despite

its small size, Pont-l'Evêque has so many fine residences. The square tower of the large church of Saint-Michel, in the flamboyant style, looks down over the town, severely damaged during the Normandy landings. Flaubert, some of whose family lived at Pont-l'Evêque, gave a detailed description of the town's architectural heritage in A simple heart. Remarkably enough, the post-war reconstruction succeeded in retaining much of the historic flavour of the original. The solemn grandeur of the Place du Tribunal, which now seems distinctly out

of place, is clear evidence of the high rank this town once held, and which is symbolized by the walls of pink brick and cut stone behind which the archives of the viscounty of Auge were stored in the 16th century. Streets with old façades opening on to courtyards or saddlers workshops stretch away along the Yvie, while visitors have, for the past five hundred years, been staying at the Auberge de l'Aigle d'Or, whose rooms are ringed by an overhanging gallery. The walls of the Hôtel Montpensier and the Hôtel de Brilly, both built in the 18th century, display the colourful blend of bricks and stone ties which was much in favour among dignitaries of the Ancien Régime.

Out in the countryside, a few rows of these stores, which contrast so nicely with a brick or halftimbered façade and so rare in the Auge region, sufficed to transform a large farmhouse, elevating it to the rank of manor. Together with genuine châteaux, there are over a hundred of these prestigious country houses along the Touques Valley, between the sea and Lisieux.

This town, founded at the point where the Touques ceased to be navigable, is the geographic and economic pole of the area. Lisieux's origins go back much further than that, as it was the capital of the Lexovii at the beginning of the Christian era and was the seat of a bishopric as early as the 6th century. In fact two church councils were held there before Henri II Plantagenêt married Aliénor of Aquitaine – an event which marked the birth, in these parts, of a great kingdom with strong imperial overtones. Having been taken, liberated, fortified and opened

Above and right:
*"And the fruits shall deliver
the promise of the blossom".*

Left, top:
*Apple trees in bloom both adorn
and symbolize Normandy
in springtime.*

Right, bottom:
Old bottles of calvados.

up, Lisieux managed to survive to June 1944, which devastated its exceptional stock of wooden houses. Work was already under way at that time on the monumental basilica of Sainte-Thérèse which rather overwhelms the local skyline.

Having taken the Carmelite veil at the age of fifteen, Sister Theresa of the Child Jesus climbed straight to the very pinnacle of mysticism, making her short life a model of sanctity. The pilgrimage to her tomb began soon after her death in 1897, and she was canonized by the Vatican in 1925. The construction of the Romano-Byzantine basilica which towers over the city started shortly thereafter. The enormous size of Sainte-Thérèse, one of the biggest of all 20th century churches, is commensurated with the magnitude of the crowds which have been devotedly attending it since its consecration in 1954.

Visitors who find the controversial architecture of the basilica not to their liking can turn their attention to a number of buildings which escaped destruction in the war, particularly the church of Saint-Pierre, the former cathedral, built in the 12th and 13th centuries. The Palais de Justice (Law Courts) located behind it, was once the Bishop's Palace; it is best known for its Salle Dorée (Gilded Room) which is hung with Cordovan leather beneath a magnificent coffered ceiling.

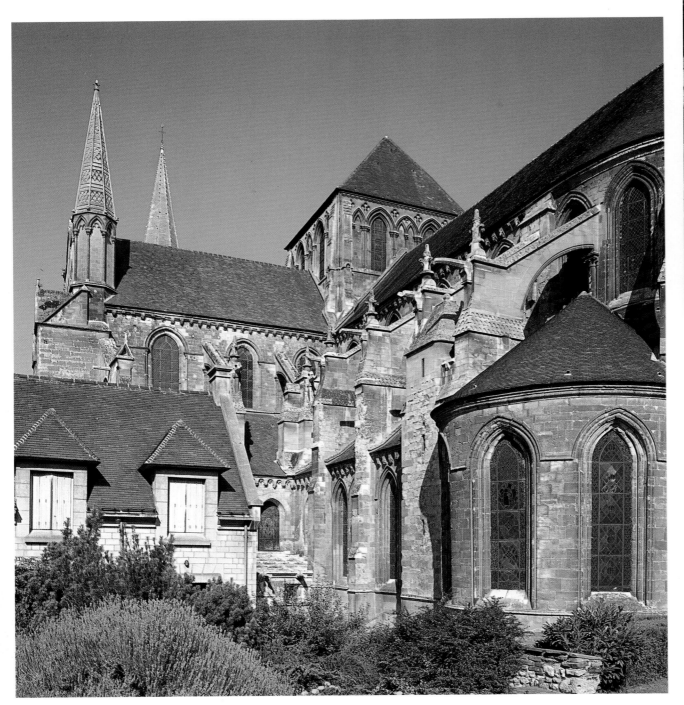

Above:
Victot-Pontfol Manor.

Facing page:
*The cathedral of St-Pierre
at Lisieux.*

Right:
*The basilica of Ste-Thérèse
at Lisieux.*

Following pages:
*Façades of manor houses
in the Auge region.*

MANORS AND CHEESES

A powerful aroma rather disconcerting for the unitiated, a soft consistency, a slightly salty flavour and the curious nickname of "colonel", which derives from the five straw binders in which it is wrapped during the hundred days of its ripening: this is Livarot, the prince of Norman cheeses in the Pont-l'Evêque area. Connoisseurs even claim that it is their king.

As for Camembert, a description is hardly necessary these days, on account of its universal success; but at one time, in the distant past, it too was a rare gastronomic treat, made by hand, before it became democratized by the growth of the dairy industry. The modern version of this local cheese was developed in the last century by Marie Harel, a farmer's wife to whom the quiet village of Camembert owes its worldwide celebrity. These products are made in the southern part of the Auge region, around Vimoutiers, where the woodlands known as the bocage cover the steeper slopes leading up to the Perche hills.

Like the upper reaches of the Touques, this valley is home to some of the most remarkable Norman manors. Surrounded by trees and water-filled moats, and standing on an feudal knoll overlooking the "royal road" from Lisieux to Bayeux, Crèvecœur-en-Auge still looks as much like a fortress as it did in its early days, with the additional charm of timbered walls and an exceptional

Above:
Half-timbered houses, apple trees and rolling meadows. The essence of Normandy, in the Camembert area.

Top:
The famous cheese in the process of being refined.

Facing page:
Bellou Manor.

square dovecote from the 15th century. The museum describes the merits of Norman architecture, curiously combined with the history of oil prospecting, whose technology was tested experimentally in this region by the Schlumberger brothers. Grandchamp, situated on a tributary of the Vie, is an even more varied mixture of periods and building materials, and includes a remarkable timbered pavilion whose four stories look down over a French garden. Coupesarte, a few miles upstream, is a spectacular sight, rising behind broad moats in which its overhanging corner turrets cast a rippling reflection. It is hard to imagine a dwelling more purely Norman than this old fort, which has been so cleverly con-

Coupesarte Manor.
Detail of the façade.

verted into a manor with a clearly agricultural function.

The Château of Fervaques, where Chateaubriand stayed a number of times on the invitation of his devoted friend Delphine de Custine, is located several miles to the west of Coupesarte; it is actually situated in the middle of the River Touques. Quite probably the most charming building in the whole Auge region is the miniature château of Saint-Germain-de-Livet, located to the north on the way to Lisieux. La Varende called it "a little jewel for a child-princess". The truth is that one can hardly believe one's eyes on first catching sight of this astonishing façade covered with an irregular grid pattern of green, pink and ochre varnished Pré-d'Auge tiles, together with brick, white stone and a timbered dwelling.

Orbec, situated at the edge of the Ouche region, near the sources of the Orbiquet, which forms one of the most pleasant valleys in these parts as it flows towards the Touques, is a delightful town whose artistic heritage and past prosperity are still very much in evidence. The Renaissance is represented by the church of Notre-Dame, its three naves covered with wood vaulting, and the Vieux Manoir, with its richly sculpted wood panelling; the opulence of the city during the classical period is demonstrated by a number of lavish townhouses.

The outer confines of the Auge region are marked by Saint-Pierre-sur-Dives, which used to be a big market trading with the grain-growing plains of Caen and Falaise, and at the same time a major monastic center. Saint-Pierre also happens to figure prominently in the production of cheese, since it manufactures most of the round or square boxes which are the setting in which these short-lived gems of Normandy are wrapped. Every Monday the large medieval covered market-place is filled with people buying and selling assorted produces.

HOULGATE AND CABOURG:
THE FRAGRANCE OF THE PAST

A whole constellation of resorts stretches along the Côte Fleurie beyond Deauville, wherever the coastline dips to accomodate them.

Some of them are eclipsed by that star of brightest magnitude shining on the Touques estuary, but at least two of them, Houlgate and Cabourg, have managed to win themselves a place in the summer firmament. Sometimes the cliffs are set back from the coast, as is the case with the twin resorts of Bénerville-Blonville, with their quiet family beaches; but they also jut out into the sea, as when they form the famous Vaches Noires Cliffs, a paradise for fossile-hunters. At this point the Auberville Plateau, where numerous campgrounds are located, sweeps down towards the shore across a lunar landscape; when seen from the sea, the boulders which now lie covered with seaweed on the beach, and which were once located far uphill, look remarkably like huge sleeping cows. This heap of stone marks the end of the long beach of Villers-sur-Mer.

Dives-sur-Mer, now a busy industrial town, was cut off from the sea by the silting up of the estuary, as a result of which its harbour gradually found itself surrounded by marshland. The town, named after the river flowing through it, used to be a major port of call, which was made eternally famous when William the Conqueror sailed from there on his victorious invasion of England. Dives-sur-Mer also cultivates these memories, with its hostelry dedicated to William the Conqueror, a railway station turned into a luxury hotel, frequented by some very distinguished people, before being converted quite recently into a cluster of art and craft boutiques. The old part of town, slightly away from the river, also includes the Bois-Hibou Manor and a superb oak-beamed covered market which contrasts starkly with the metal-working factories along the banks of the Dives and indeed the villas and the grid-pattern avenues of Cabourg.

Above:
Dives-sur-Mer. The hostelry of William the Conqueror.

Left:
Dives-sur-Mer. The church of Notre-Dame.

Right:
The House of the Fishermen, at Houlgate.

Following pages:
Houlgate. A most delightful setting, with its vast sandy beach and beautiful sea wall promenade. Houlgate has always been a highly popular seaside resort.

The history of this resort is as its semi-circular layout, centered about its main driving force – the Casino and the Grand-Hôtel. At this spot, where the young Duke of Normandy had already distinguished himself by driving the troops of French Henri I into the sea, the landscape consisted merely of dunes and lagoons, with a few fishermen's cottages. In 1860 promoters moved in, hoping to make a fortune from the application of the same formula which had succeeded so well at Trouville, and built the seaside resort of Cabourg from the ground up. The director of a number of Parisian theatres and their actors did much to bring about its success.

Since then, the town has changed little; indeed a walk along its streets takes one straight back into the world of Proust's navet, Within a Budding Grove, set in the imaginary resort of Balbec. The Promenade des Anglais has been renamed in honour of this eminent local figure, who continued to visit the resort loyally from 1907 to 1914, having first discovered it as a child. The atmosphere invites one to see things again through the novelist's eyes, to visualize the broad shaded avenues, converging in their fan-shaped pattern on the Grand-Hôtel.

CAEN, CITY
OF WILLIAM
AND MATHILDE

**Before going to war
to secure his claim
to the throne
of England, William
had had recourse
to somewhat
similar methods
in his courtship of
Mathilde of Flanders.**

At first the lad resisted his entreaties, stating "I would rather take the veil than be wed to a bastard", whereupon the duke, who was no ordinary suitor, forced his way into her palace and dragged her off forcibly. His approach clearly worked, as the marriage, which was celebrated shortly thereafter, was a lasting and happy one. However, the couple was left for a number of years with a major headache: the fact that their distant kinship, as cousins, for which they had not requested a papal dispensation, meant that they were excommunicated from the Church. It was not until the successor of Hellouin, the famous Lanfranc, interceded on their behalf, that the pope lifted his ban; but the resulting penance was quite severe – William and Mathilde were required to build four hospitals and two abbeys.

At the time, William had already chosen as the seat of his duchy the small port of Caen, where work was already under way on the construction of his castle. So he decided to enhance it further by fulfilling part of his penance there; Queen Mathilde followed suit. With the Abbaye-aux-Hommes and the Abbay-aux-Dames

situated on either side of the fortress, the city became increasingly grand – a trend which continued under the Conqueror's descendants. Many centuries later Caen, which had since those times been the capital of Lower Normandy, also found itself on the stage of History, when it was almost flattened during the Allied landings during the second World War. Reconstruction made it possible to highlight the main elements of its legacy, in particular a distinctive style and a famous type of stone to which the duke-king was so attached that he had it used in the building of Canterbury Cathedral, Westminster Abbey and the Tower of London.

Work began on the church of Saint-Etienne, in the Abbaye-aux-Hommes, in 1063 and was completed only fourteen years later; such remarkable speed accounts for its homogeneity. Its first abbot was Lanfranc, later to be Archbishop of Canterbury, and the stark majesty of the façade can be ascribed to that prelate's Lombard origins. At the beginning of the 13th century discreet Gothic belfries were added to the square towers, and the apse was remodelled in the new style, thus

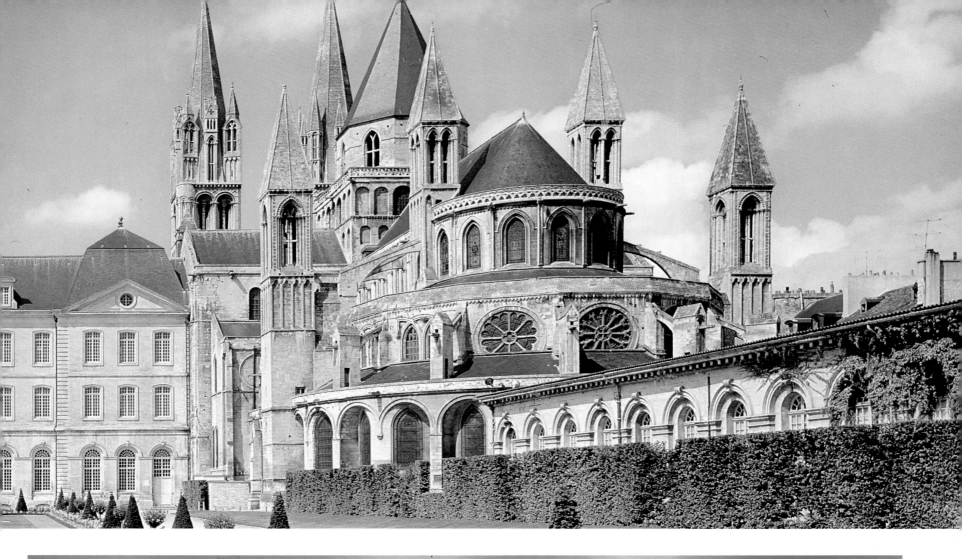

becoming the first of its kind in Normandy.

The monastery buildings of the Benedictines adjoining the church were rebuilt in 1704, at the same time as those of the Abbaye-aux-Dames, and now retain nooneGothic features except for the Guard Room. This long façade, whose rigor is attributable to

the austerity of the congregation of Saint-Maur, blends harmoniously with the chevet of the church. The building is now occupied by the Caen town hall.

The Abbaye-aux-Dames, constructed under the supervision of Mathilde, to whom William had entrusted the affairs of the duchy

while he was away engaged in conquest, lacks the soaring inspiration of its male counterpart; though it does have a greater abundance of decorative work, based on geometric patterns which emigrated to the rest of Normandy and to England. The church of the Trinity follows the Benedictine plan, with apsidal chapels and a semi-dome apse around the choir where Queen Mathilde lies buried.

Caen is blessed with an abundance of chapels, ranging from the completely intact Romanesque chapel of Saint-Nicolas to the concrete lacework of Saint-Julien, which was rebuilt after the war, though special reference should be made to Saint-Pierre, which encapsulates four centuries of architecture in the spirited tumult of its fine stonework – a spectacle which, to the rich bourgeoisie of Caen, must have seemed like a reflection of its own prosperity. Pride of place among the dwellings of the affluent merchant class must surely

go to the Hôtel d'Escoville, a prominent representative of Renaissance in the region.

William the Conqueror's favorite castle, that stands opposite Saint-Pierre and the Hôtel d'Escoville now displays its full power, after the reconstruction of the city succeeded in providing a clear view of the huge original fortifications, which were heavily remodelled in the 14th century. Scattered about a public garden inside the fortified outer walls there are a number of structures which warrant a special mention. These are, from an architectural point of view, the chapel of Saint-Georges, and the Hall of the Exchequer, as well as the Governor's House, now the Normandy Museum; the well-endowed Fine Art Museum is housed in a modern building. Their various collections of the highest quality show how the capital of Lower Normandy has always been a major focal point for culture – a role it now continues to play through its renowned university.

Though much of Caen was rebuilt from the ground up after the devastation of 1944, or perhaps for that very reason, it is a well-designed city with numerous pedestrian streets; it is also unusual in that it allows both countryside and sea to penetrate far within its walls: the Prairie between the Orne and the Odon is a huge green space partly occupied by the race track – a reminder that harness racing began here. Similarly, Saint-Pierre dock, a former commercial harbour now used by pleasure crafts, is evidence of Caen's maritime vocation, which is now concentrated along the Orne Canal.

Above:
Caen: the castle walls.

Right:
The Maison des Quatrans.

Facing page:
Caen: part of the modern city.

BAYEUX AND THE QUEEN MATHILDE TAPESTRY

"A very long and narrow piece of fabric embroidered with inscriptions and images depicting the conquest of England", were the words used in an inventory of 1476.

"A comic strip is the thought that comes to mind, in our modern image-based civilization, when one first sees the famous Bayeux Tapestry, a monumental piece of needlework dating from the period shortly after the victory of William the Conqueror. If the fact that an 11th century church, for example, could have survived the passages of many centuries unscathed still seems astonishing to us, then what can one possibly say about this embroidery of colored wool on linen, all 231 feet of it, still decorated with its eight bright or pastel shades, telling the story of a little-known period? It was perhaps inevitable for tradition to take over, introducing the notion of a latter-day Penelope – Queen Mathilde – awaiting the return of her warrior husband; the truth,

Above:
An early votive offering, the "Glories of Mary".

Right:
The famous Tapestry of Queen Mathilde.

Facing page:
The choir of Bayeux Cathedral.

however, is more down-to-earth, even though it does directly involve the Conqueror. This fresco was probably commissioned by Odon de Conteville, William's half-brother, who was Bishop of Bayeux and the new Duke of Kent, from a studio in Canterbury. This background sheds an interesting new light on the interpretation of the tapestry, which, besides being a chronicle glorifying the victor, is to an equal extent a moral tale, seeking to edify the faithful by showing them how the death of the perfidious Harold was just punishment for his earlier perjury. Leaving this aspect aside, however, the modern viewer can enjoy the simple pleasure of seeing history told with humour and poetry, its protagonists clearly identifiable (smooth faces and shaved necks for the Normans; beards and moustaches for the English) and the whole story told with outstanding esthetic skill and striking authenticity. For this reason also historians take endless delight in studying the tapestry – an exceptional source of information about such matters as dress, cavalry, ships or daily life in the new millenium.

In 1077 the "canvas of the Conquest" was completed in time for the dedication of the cathedral, built under the auspices of the same Odon, who besides being a leading ecclesiastical figure, was also a lively companion-in-arms of Duke William. This was a great moment in Norman history, a bond with the past recorded in the presence of all the dignitaries of the duchy and the new kingdom on the far side of the Channel. Bayeux also played a part in the birth of the Norman state, as Rolf the Marcher, after storming the town in 911, married Popa, daughter of Count Béranger, the defeated governor; from that union William Longsword was born, an ancestor of William the Conqueror. After its initial display in the presence of the duke-king, the tapestry was hung around the choir of the church once a year for the next four hundred years, drawing crowds from the far ends of the province. The building we see today, much renovated during the 19th century, when it also acquired its copper roof, bears little resemblance to the 11th century cathedral, which was heavily damaged by fire before being restored in the Gothic style.

The city itself, formerly the capital of the Bessin region, has a great

deal of personality, having managed to avoid both industrialization and battle damage from the Second World War, despite the proximity of the beaches on which the Allies landed. It still retains something of the gentle atmosphere of the city of clerks, bourgeois and ecclesiastics it used to be during the last century; and it is still quite close to the bocage, runing along the edge of its boulevards, as can be seen from the picturesque Saturday market on the Place Saint-Patrice. Apart from the old houses on the streets adjacent to the cathedral and the seminary which has now been converted in order to accomodate the famous tapestry, Bayeux has two interesting museums: the one devoted to the Battle of Normandy supplements the presentation at Arromanches, by giving a detailed account of the fighting which took place in the bocage immediately after the landings, and recording the resulting devastation. The Baron-Gérard Museum, besides its assorted collections, has on display a number of exhibits illustrating historical specimens of the work of local craftsmen, particularly in lace and porcelain.

The brilliant dynasty founded by Rolf was always generous towards the Bessin, first and foremost by rebuilding the places of worship destroyed by the Vikings. As a further example, in 1032 Robert the Magnificent restored the past splendour of the abbey of Cerisy-la-Forêt, in the heart of the Bessin region. Although it has since lost its Benedictines and four of its transepts, the abbey church is one of the best preserved in Normandy; seen from the chevet it displays a power and a soaring majesty which testify eloquently to the power of the dukes.

Mondaye Abbey, situated closer to Bayeux, was founded in 1212 by the Premonstratensians; the present buildings, in a flawlessly classical style, still house a monastic community which excels in the production of cheese.

There are fewer manor houses in the Bessin than in the Auge region, but it does have a number of remarkable châteaux, the main one being Balleroy. This is no mere château in the usual sense, as the village itself

was used to highlight this masterpiece in its grand setting at the end of the only street, which is as broad as an avenue. With architecture by François Mansart and flowerbeds and landscaping by his accomplice André Le Nôtre, Balleroy represents the best of the Louis XIV period among the foliage of Normandy – a scene which is sometimes given an additional splash of colour when hot-air balloon rallies are being held nearby.

Lastly, along the edge of the Caen Plain, one should spend some time visiting Creully, and in particular Fontaine-Henry, the gem of the Caen Renaissance; one can follow the development of that style from one façade to the next, beneath the immense pointed roof, which is about twice the height of the Grand Pavillon.

Above:
Brécy: the small church, the castle and the terraced gardens.

Top:
Balleroy Castle.

Facing page:
The château of Fontaine-Henry.

Left, top:
The "stele" at Hoc Pointe.

Left, bottom:
Views of Ouistreham.

Facing page:
The cliffs at Port-en-Bessin.

THE D-DAY BEACHES, FROM THE ORNE TO THE VIRE

More than forty years elapsed since the fighting took place along the Calvados coast, but it still is keenly remembered.

Even though the wounds caused by this turning point in history have now healed, the scars remain, in the form of war cemeteries consisting of thousands of white crosses stretching away into the distance, sharp subsidences made by bomb craters, bunkers and casemates, or the ruined caissons of the man-made harbour at Arromanches. The tourist visiting the Mother of Pearl Coast (Côte de Nacre) and the Bassin coast is treated to some strange contrasts, moving from memorial to family beach, from Langrune, a Viking name, to Sword Beach and other places also named after their D-Day codes. Between Merville and Courseulles, however, developers promoting seaside resorts have done their utmost to relegate these wartime memories to the background; but they continue to exert a powerful hold on the imagination along the bocage, the beaches and the cliffs of the Bessin.

Immediately after Cabourg the Normandy coast changes both its name and its appearance: the only landmarks along the Mother-of-Pearl Coast are the village belfries, while treacherous shoals just offshore, only a short distance from long and wide beaches, lie hidden beneath the waves. One such shoal, near Arromanches, proved fatal to the Salvador, one of the ships of the invincible Spanish Armada, and the corrupted form of its name was adopted as the title of the department of Calvados. There are only two ports along this stretch of exceedingly flat coastline: Ouistreham, near the River Orne, and Courseulles on the Seulles; elsewhere, the waves roll out a carpet of seaweed, whose unmistakable smell is noticeable at low tide, in front of houses whose walls, instead of being timbered, are built with the beautiful Caen stone.

The mouth of the Orne marked the eastern end of Operation Overlord, on 6th June 1944; indeed the first hostil-

ities took place in this key sector into which British airborne commandos were dropped at midnight. Their mission was to take intact both Ranville and Bénouville bridges, which have since then been renamed Pegasus Bridge, in honour of the emblem of the Sixth Airborne Division; they also were given the difficult task of neutralizing the big guns at Merville-Franceville. Reminders of this high point in the D-Day landings are strewn about the landscape of the estuary: museums, cemeteries, monuments and military fortifications which have not been completely submerged in the huge seaside resort complex of modern Ouistreham and Riva-Bella. These two towns thus combine the advantages of a large marina situated at the exit from the Caen Canal and those of the finest beach in the area.

At Courseulles a Sherman tank stands guard at the entrance to the harbour, which was crucial for the Allies, pending the completion of the manmade dock at Arromanches. Winston Churchill, General de Gaulle and King George VI set foot here in mid-June, when all the troops engaged in the battle of Normandy had joined forces. This old fishing harbour, traditionally renowned for the quality of the locally-grown oysters, has since become a favorite port of call with pleasure crafts. Thereafter the coast begins to rise. Its rare sea-level openings provided welcome beachheads for the soldiers of the Liberation, though they did not make it possible to move inland the thousands of tons of vehicles, hardware and supplies necessary for the success of the landings. This gave rise to the strategists' daring idea of building two large-capacity manmade harbours on this inhospitable coast. The one at Vierville was destroyed by a storm on June 19th, but Arromanches found its way into the history books, thanks to the remaining Mulberry harbour – one of the most remarkable accomplishment of the last world war. Sixty ships were scuttled to form a first breakwater, and then a hundred and forty six monstruous concrete caissons, together with ten miles of pontoon roads to serve as wharves and jetties!

The American sectors of Omaha and Utah Beach start a short distance further on; the past comes flooding back, with poignant memories carved

Above:
Sainte-Mère-Eglise: the church and a Roman military milestone.

Left:
The cemetery of Colleville-sur-Mer.

Facing page:
A room in the farm-museum of Le Cotentin.

into this forbidding landscape. The Atlantic Wall, with its massive fortifications, towers over a narrow and bare beach. There was a huge slaughter of soldiers and Ranger commandos who found themselves reduced to primitive methods in order to reach the plateau at Hoc Point. Using grappling hooks and rope ladders they fought their way through a wall of steel and fire. This was the scene of the deadliest fighting in the whole Battle of Normandy; the earth, laid waste by explosions, was further pitted with the graves of thousands of American and German soldiers.

The Allied success was in part due to the sheer disbelief which greeted their landing on such unfavourable shores; indeed the Germans thought for a while that the real invasion was taking place somewhere else. Between Courseulles and the Vire there was really only one tiny harbour which could link the bocage of the Bessin and the sea, since at that time Grandcamp was nothing more than a haven for fishing boats.

THE BOCAGES NEAR SAINT-LÔ AND THE VIRE VALLEY

While the Rangers had reinstated a number of age-old methods to claw their way up the cliffs of the D-Day beaches, the soldiers of the Wehrmacht were not found wanting in this respect, either: in the bocage they fell back on the guerilla tactics of the Chouans, who rebelled in western France during the Revolution, in order to pin down the allied armored forces in what came to be known as the Battle of the Hedgerows.

Facing American troops who could not find their way around a totally unfamiliar landscape, these infantrymen made the fullest possible use of each plot of land, hiding scrub and confronting the tank crews with a difficult choice: they could get bogged down along very narrow sunken roads, or they could try to scale the embankments, thus running the risk of exposing the weak points of their armour to enemy fire. As heavy artillery was ineffective in such an environment, it took the GIs weeks to mop up the bocage, methodically, orchard by orchard, hedge by hedge, until July 12th, when they finally reached the heights of Saint-Lô, the prefecture of the department of the Manche. Then the effects of the dreadful bombings inflicted on the town since the landings were compounded by new fighting. The German command had turned this crossroads into a strong point in their defenses, with which they intended to halt their Allies: it fell one week later, but another week was required, together with a massive pounding, before the front yielded to any real extent in this sector, and Patton's tanks were able to break through into the bocage.

After the war, Saint-Lô was quickly rebuilt around the Enclos, its historic core, situated on a schist outcropping above the river, which Charlemagne had girdled with ramparts. A pleasant shaded promenade along the former site of the walls, past two towers – Porte-au-Lait and Beauregard – enables the visitor to see the reconstructed city. Apart from the church of Notre-Dame and its fine stained glass windows, Saint-Lô has an interesting Fine Arts Museum. Also famous for its studfarm, which includes a large number of purebred stallions, Saint-Lô is a prime center for the breeding of French trotters and racehorses; teams of horses perform spectacular displays here each summer, after the major equestrian events of Ascension Week, when more than five hundred horses take part in competitions.

The Saint-Lô bocage, which suffered much less damage in the war than the city itself, has an abundance of varied tourist attractions, in addition to certain scenic beauties such as granite cliffs of the Ham Rocks, which overhang the meandering River Vire. A number of fine country houses are dotted about these hills, and the farmhouses themselves are graced by superb stonework centuries old, while the châteaux sometimes take on a rustic air, as in the case of Angotière, which has a big dovecote and thatched outbuildings. Montfort, Castel, Cerisy-la-Salle and many others lie nestled among the most beautiful settings in the bocage, though they cannot rival the renown of the château of Torigni-sur-Vire, birthplace of the famous Robert de Torigni, who was abbot of Mont-Saint-Michel in the 12th century. The present building dates from the end of the reign of Henry IV.

Above:
La Vire, at Ham Rocks.

Right:
Villedieu-les-Poêles: the center of the village.

In Calvados, in the upper part of the valley and in another bocage, Vire stands in a defensive position above the Vaux de Vire, a place mentioned in various drinking songs and which eventually gave rise to the term vaudeville. Like Saint-Lô, this strategic bridge was destroyed during the Liberation, but its principal pieces of architecture, the Clock Tower and the church of Notre-Dame, have been restored in the superb and slightly yellow granite characteristic of this region, which is itself crossbred with Brittany. However the region is much more famous for its pork sausage, which is as well known as tripe in Caen and black pudding in Mortagne.

The local specialities have a following outside France, but certainly not in as many places around the world as the products of one small town in the Manche, which are enjoyed all over the world every day. These are, of course, the brass bells whose secret has been known to Villedieu-les-Poêles for the past nine centuries. The son of William-the-Conqueror had granted these lands to the Hospitaller Brothers of Saint John of Jerusalem, and Villedieu was one of the order's first commanderies. Their small foundry attracted craftsmen and a number of privileges incided them to settle here; since then, copper has always been beaten and bells always cast in the town, whose distinctly medieval character was not altered by the last war.

THE LAND OF THE LAST VIKINGS

The Peninsula of Normandy, the Cotentin, is similar in many ways with Brittany: a marine climate, its peasants farming seaweed, a multitude of small harbours and a rather rocky landscape.

In fact, however, the Cotentin Peninsula is not Celtic at all – it is really the most Scandinavian part of Normandy, the only one inhabited by persons of Norwegian, as well as the more customary Danish extraction; the names of practically all the villages bear testimony of these origins. Almost as if this prow of the continent, braving the waves and winds of the open sea, had inspired them, the Normans of the Cotentin Peninsula set off for foreign lands, not just collectively to England, accompanying their duke, but also individually. Between 1030 and 1130, on the pretext of fighting Byzantium, they founded the countships of Aversa and Apulia, the principalities of Capua and Antioch, and also the kingdom of Sicily. This was a sport at which the sons of Tancrède de Hauteville, a baron from near Coutances, excelled: the eldest, William, was a mercenary who chose to be called Iron Arm; it

Left, top:
The Hôtel de Beaumont, at Valognes.

Left, bottom:
The port of St-Vaast-la-Hougue.

Facing page:
The valley of Saire, view from the hill of La Pernelle. In the background, the island of Tatihou, with its citadel and dungeon.

was he who, outwitting his employers, seized Apulia. Roger and Robert, who had come to offer him their support, later shared the south of Italy and Sicily which, under the rule of the Norman kings, experienced one of the most prosperous periods in their history, represented by enormous cathedrals such as those of Palermo and Cefalu. The Viking spirit was to disappear altogether after this period, but a new blood was now circulating in many parts of Europe, and with it the Norman passion for building.

The hinterland of the peninsula consists of woodlands, the bocage, similar to those of the Bessin, though they are separated by huge stretches of marsh. Throughout the centuries, Valogne, the natural crossroads of this area, has been the marketplace of the region and a major center for the dairy and lumber business; it has unfortunately lost much of the proud bearing it had as an aristocratic capital before the bombing of 1944. We are reminded of those days by Barbey d'Aurevilly, the nineteenth century writer who sang the peninsula's praises, though he did not himself witness the splendour of the closing

days of the Ancien Régime. In those days the hundred noblest families of the town used to hold brilliant courts, each in its own mansion, thus making Valognes a kind of Norman Versailles. The Hôtel de Beaumont, the most outstanding among them, was spared as well as the Hôtel de Granval-Caligny, where the Constable of Letters used to reside.

After Veys Bay, formerly the site of the fords which linked the Cotentin Peninsula to the Bessin, the coast is sandy, with the dunes and the set-back marshes which the second Armored Division, having come ashore at Varreville, had some difficulty in crossing. Offshore we see the first of the Channel Islands, the Marcouf Islands, which have been abandoned by man for the tranquillity of the seabirds; the forts in which they nest remind us that the waters of history have swirled about Saint-Vaast-la-Hougue. Great fleets of warships did, in fact, sail quite close to the walls of this peaceful fishing port, with a Flemish name given it by the people of Fécamp, which is also well known for its oysters, beaches and mimosas. First came the landing of the English, at the beginning of the

Hundred Years' War; then the disastrous Battle of La Hougue, in 1692, in which the ships under the command of Tourville about to invade England were destroyed by the Anglo-Dutch fleet.

The oldest port on this section of the Cotentin coast is Barfleur, not far from one of the two points off the shores of the peninsula where the currents are particularly dangerous. The prime location of this protected haven soon made Barfleur a bridge head for later conflicts between France and England – a most unfortunate position to be in, as history showed. Although the local fisheries did pick up somewhat after the Revolution, Barfleur never recovered again the splendour it had known in the Middle Ages, and has since then turned inwards, sleepily, on its own past. This is just the kind of drowsy tranquillity, against the background of old granite houses with schist roofs clustered about the square belfry of the church, down by the water, that many summer visitors simply love. The violent currents, that swirl to and fro just offshore, were the reason for the construction, in the 19th century, of a rescue station, which

has an impressive record to its credit, and also one of the tallest lighthouses in France, from where there is an impressive view of the coastline. The view from the top reminds one of Brittany – nothing but rocky reefs fringed with foam, trees kept low by the wind and the rocky ledges along the coast.

On the other hand, the Saire Valley which forms the hinterland of this part of the peninsula, seems almost exaggeratedly Norman. Like the coast, the hamlets in this valley have been spared the ugliness which lax zoning has brought to some vacations areas; here the bocage, well away from the most heavily traveled tourist circuits, has preserved its farmhouses, its manors, its mills and its churches.

Top and facing page:
Two views of Barfleur.

A CITY IN THE HEART OF THE MANCHE REGION: CHERBOURG

Everyone acknowledged the need to make Cherbourg a major naval base; but it had first to be protected from the open sea – a titanic venture which involved building a manmade roadstead between Querqueville and Bretteville, a distance of five miles.

In keeping with the plans of Captain De La Bretonnière, the first wooden caissons loaded with rock were sunk in the middle of the bay in the presence of Louis XVI. On land the construction of the forts of Querqueville, Le Homet and Pelée Island were progressing satisfactorily, but work on the dike was exasperatingly slow, as both winds and currents seemed to conspire to destroy whatever had been built. Hard work and determination were the sole solutions the engineers could devise; so that three-quarters of a century went by before the great dike was completed. In the meantime Napoleon I had been able to excavate the docks of the naval harbour, which were finished by Napoleon III; in 1830 the commercial dock was opened and the great transatlantic liners then began to call

at Cherbourg, which equipped itself with a mainline rail connection to the docks. Luckily the harbour had been designed on a truly grand scale, so that in 1944, after the port had been cleared of wreckage and freed of mines, Cherbourg was able to supply on its own all the allied armies as they pressed on inland; oil was pumped across the channel through PLUTO, the Pipe Line Under The Ocean.

The coming of peace did not deter the city from performing its new functions; indeed business generated by the arsenal helped offset the economic weakness of the hinterland; the docks are a hive of activity with the various cross-Channel connections, the container traffic, the flow of yachts and trawlers. In the naval harbour the arsenal is involved in the construction of nuclear submarines and small specialized units, such as fast motor launches. Rouke Fort, on high ground overlooking the city, is a perfect vantage point from which to take in the maze of docks surrounding the small roadstead, which is in turn protected from the open sea by the dike. This fort, which was the hub of German resistance, also has a Museum of the War and the Liberation. In town, one should make a visit to the Fine Arts Museum: the well-stocked exhibit of paintings includes, in particular, some thirty canvases by Jean-François Millet, who was born

locally. The presence of tropical species in the delightful Emmanuel-Liais Park, next to the Museum of Natural Sciences, also worth a visit, demonstrates the beneficent effect of the Gulf Stream at these latitudes. Other sights include Voeu Abbey, now being restored, the Flamboyant basilica of La Trinité, facing the Place Napoléon.

Towards La Hague Point, where the fastest currents to be found on any French coast occur, at Blanchard Race, the coastline becomes increasingly wild until it reaches the most rugged part of all, the Nez de Jobourg, the Norman counterpart of Brittany's Raz Point. There can be few places in Normandy which have inspired so many terrifying legends, some containing an element of truth, because smugglers and ship wreckers used to abound in these parts.

At Querqueville there is a charming pre-Romanesque church, Saint-Germain. Dur-Ecu and Nacqueville, two handsome 16th century manors, are situated in the beautiful countryside around Urville, and then the road leads to Gréville, home of Millet. The villages become increasingly intimate, like Omonville-la-Rogue, which is as rustic and inviting as its neighbour Omonville-la-Petite, while the tiny Port-Racine has the proud distinction of being the smallest French harbour...

Above:
Port-Racine – the smallest port in France.

Top:
Landscape near Cape la Hague.

Facing page, top:
Cherbourg: the fishing harbour.

Facing page, bottom:
The rocks at Nez-de-Jobourg.

Above: *The castle of St-Sauveur-le-Vicomte.*

Top: *The manor of St-Martin-le-Mébort.*

Facing page, top: *The abbey of Notre-Dame-de-Grâce, at Bricquebec.*

Facing page, bottom: *The fortified church of Portbail.*

WESTERN COTENTIN PENINSULA: INLETS AND WETLANDS

On the far side of La Hague, the outermost tip of Normandy, a number of scenic openings occur in the western façade of the Cotentin Peninsula, a prelude to the rather special coastline runing from Carteret to Granville.

The first few bays, which still have something of the austerity of the great headland itself, are the solitary beach at Ecalgrain, bordering on moors covered with heather; and then Vauville Inlet, which stretches as far as the cliffs at Flamanville. Along this perfect arc a cordon of dunes encloses a string of marshes, and the village had to be built a little way back from the shore, at the foot of a slope. This arrangement occurs frequently to the south along the costal area of inlets and wetlands (mielles) in which tidal currents and the powerful waves coming from the sea carry in sand which settled between each rocky outcropping. This filling process is fatal to the cliffs, as they lose their contours and become covered in vegetation behind the wetlands or mielles, which originally were lagoons hemmed in by the dunes. This coastal strip thus formed is often used for market-gardening, as the mild influence of the Gulf Stream is felt here too. Those rivers big enough to force their way through to the sea have created large and shallow estuaries which are

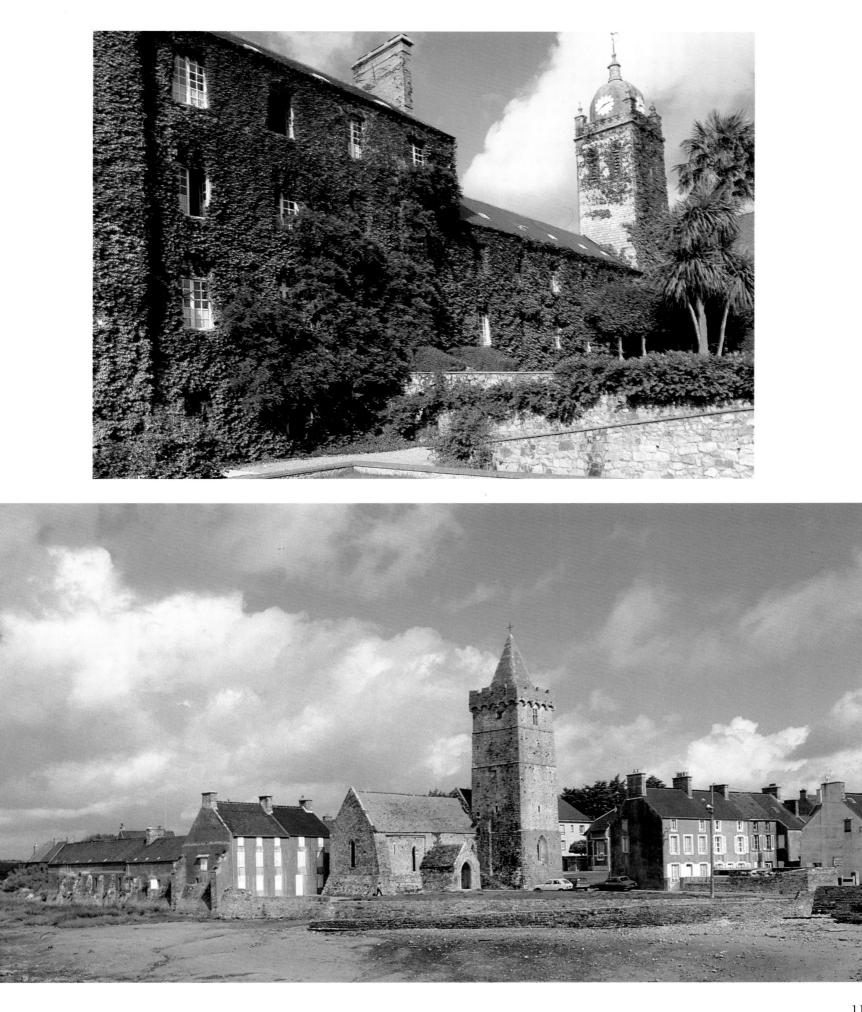

Above:
*A rustic interior
in the Coutançais region.*

Top:
*The Château des Galeries at Bricquebec
is a long single-storey Renaissance
building with wide transom windows
framed by pilasters.*

Facing page:
*The cathedral of Coutances,
with the vaulting in the nave.*

repeatedly emptied and refilled by the tides; these are the hâvres (havens), where boats occasionally enter to find shelter in rough weather. Nestling at the foot of the lifeless cliffs, the villages, in which agriculture is more important than fisheries, are linked to the shore by the tangour roads once laid for the wagons which carted in the muddy sand, a powerful fertilizer. The tourist trade is beginning to look for these long-forgotten villages, while conservation groups are doing their best to ensure that tourist development, if it takes place at all, is kept within certain strict limits – in other words, the eternal tug-of-war.

There are, however, some good and long established resorts along this part of the Normandy coast. Barneville-Carteret, a traditional port for the Channel Islands which can be seen against the setting sun beyond the Déroute Passage. The beaches of Carteret and Barneville, around a magnificent rocky headland, are among the nicest on the whole peninsula; here the deposits of sand that have led to the decline of the port have proved to be a valuable asset. The novelist Barbey d'Aurevilly, a native of the nearby village of Saint-Sauveur-le-Vicomte which he found "as pretty as a Scottish hamlet", was also fond of Carteret, where he had a country house where he occasionally withdrew from the world to forget about his work as a writer, which often involved him in polemics. The beach runs all the way from Bameville to Portbail, whose shallow protected estuary also attracts large numbers of pleasure craft. Lastly we come to the large but recent resort of Coutainville, built on an enormous barrier of dunes that protects the crescent shaped estuary from the sea; the inhabitants of Coutance naturally frequent this resort in large numbers.

Coutance, which historically has had no connection with the coast, is very much a product of the bocage. It has also been the seat of a bishopric, as can be readily perceived by the visitor on seeing the cathedral of Notre-Dame towering over the slate roofs. This is a most unusual building of the 13th century, which fits amazingly well over the remains of the church built two hundred years previously through the generosity of the son of Tancrède de Hauteville, who was away in the Mediterranean engaged in various adventures. Any hint of the massiveness of the underlying Romanesque structure is hidden by the profusion of soaring vertical lines on the façade, the scaled spires and the daring lead-covered lantern-tower known as Le Plomb. In the nave, a multitude of ribs and a skilful combination of vaulting and varying floor heights give the cathedral the same kind of elevation of which Notre-Dame in Coutances is a fine example, rather like the choir of Saint-Etienne and La Merveille (The Marvel) of Mont-Saint-Michel.

The vitality of the monastic movement in the Middle Ages also led to the construction of several other magnificent abbeys in this part of the peninsula. The architecture of the ruined church of the Premonstratensians, in Lucerne Abbey, is quite as austere as that of the Cistercians. Hambye Abbey, dating from about the same time, is still an imposing presence in the Sienne Valley, where its Romanesque lantern-tower, flanked by a Gothic choir, is a local landmark. Without any doubt, the

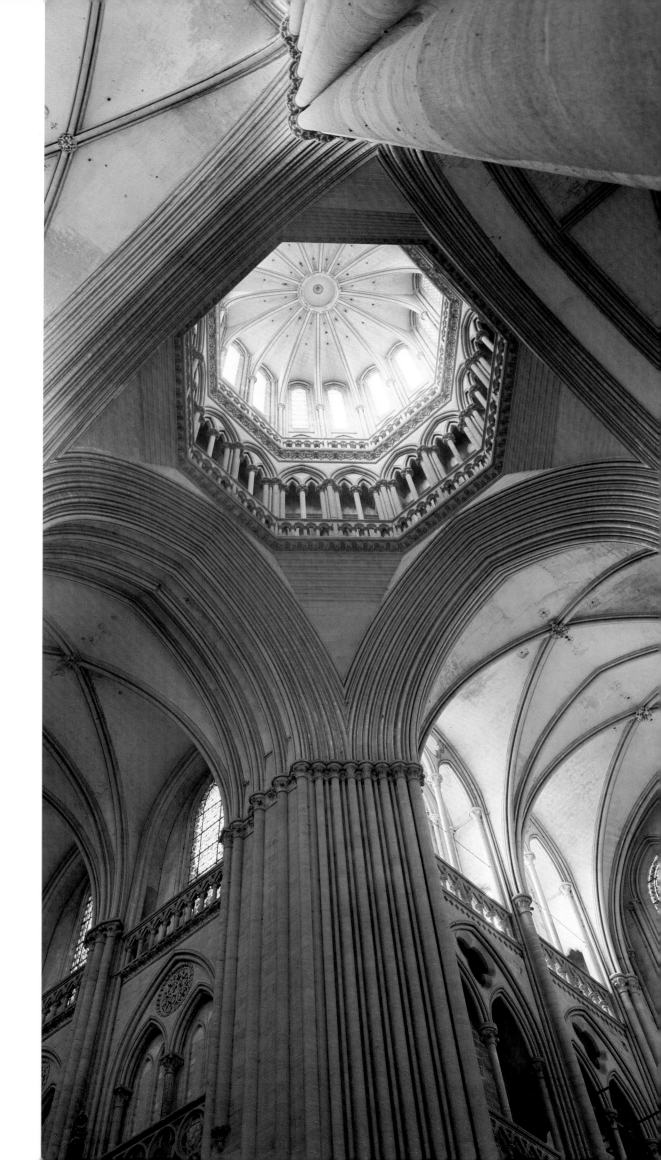

most interesting of all is the abbey church of Lessay, which has been perfectly restored: some scholars believe that its nave is the first example in history of the pointed transept. Ever since the time of that innovation, the village has been famous for it horse fair, the Grande Sainte Croix, which used to be attended by visitors from as far away as Nizhny-Novgorod, the modern Gorky, in Russia! The buyers are no longer foreign, but after the day's business is over they still enjoy themselves in exactly the same way as their predecessors by having a hearty meal of leg of lamb from the salt meadows, washed down with the best local cider.

Similar merrymaking occurs at the famous Granville Carnival, a relic of the days when the fishing fleets, before setting out for the Newfoundland banks, used to spend their advances in a matter of days.

Left:
Ruins of the abbey church of Hambye.

Top:
View of the Chausey Islands.

Facing page:
The port of Granville.

AVRANCHES, THE GUARDIAN OF MONT-SAINT-MICHEL

The destinies of Mont-Saint-Michel and Avranches, situated at the border between Normandy and Brittany, have long been interwined.

After all, Saint-Auber, who was left incredulous by the apparition of the Archangel Michael, before going on himself to build a chapel in his honour on Mount Tombe, was an archbishop of Avranches. His skull with the hole made, according to tradition, by the finger of the Archangel, who was growing impatient with Auber's vacillation, can now be seen in the treasury of the basilica of Saint-Gervais. Thereafter the influx of pilgrims towards the Mount brought considerable benefits, first of all, to Avranches, whose religious role grew considerably.

This remote rock, whose sides are swept by the strongest tides in France, was predestined to be a haven for meditation; the long saga of the Mount must have started around the year 500, when two hermits withdrew there to lead monastic life. Two centuries later, Saint-Auber dedicated this spot to Archangel Michael, and twelve canons thereafter worked there in the divine service. Then pilgrims began to arrive, everyone from tramps to kings; Childéric III was the first of the latter to come, and as it became a place of refuge in troubled times, Mont-Saint-Michel soon had

to be fortified. Spirituality suffered as a result; compliance with the monastic rule became lax and Duke Richard the Fearless, at the dawn of the year 1000, had to replace the cannons with thirty Benedictines from such backgrounds as Saint-Wandrille, Evreux or Jumièges.

The first place of worship built on the rock was a pre-Romanesque structure, Notre-Dame-Sous-Terre (Our Lady Under Ground), which was fully opened up early in the 20th century. The increase in the size of the crowds made a much bigger church a necessity, so the Benedictines built one with funds donated by the next duke, Richard the Good. As there was no room left at the top of the rock, the monks built their long Romanesque church out over three crypts secured to the rock face: Saint-Martin, Notre-Dame-des-Trente-Cierges and Les Gros Piliers, beneath the choir. The energy of these Normans is simply staggering, when one thinks that the stone they used was brought from the Chausey Islands, and that the entire project was completed in less than half a century.

When Normandy became French, Phillippe-Auguste did his best to compensate for the damage done by his Breton allies, who had succeeded in taking the Mount; his efforts led to the construction of La Merveille, one of the masterpieces of the Middle Ages, rising sheer above the gardens on the north slope.

The Hundred Years' War rather curbed the mystic vigour of the rock, when Du Guesclin took over its garrison. The new construction, though military in purpose, is nonetheless quite interesting. Eventually peace brought with it the restoration of prosperity. The collapse of the choir of the abbey church gave Gothic art an opportunity to stage one more, and this time final, display in the sky over the bay.

Left:
The cloister, a masterpiece of grace and elegance, has retained its original layout: a series of galleries open out onto the courtyard, with two parallel sets of arcades in staggered rows, resting on slender pillars.

Above:
The Mont-Saint-Michel, "the wonder of the western world", Mecca of faith, art and culture. Built on a small granite island in the most magnificent setting, the village, abbey and church rise in a pyramid-shaped cluster; the tall church spire bears the statue of Saint-Michel.

Following pages:
The famous salt-water meadows.

THE BOCAGES AT THE SOUTHERN EDGE OF NORMANDY

Referring to the bocage is a convenient way of mentioning the southwest of Normandy. When one considers the area in detail, however, it is not so simple: the bocage really does not exist as a separate concept. Instead it tends to be linked with a specific place-name, such as Vire or Saint-Lô, Avranches or Passais.

In school children are taught that the bocage consists of meadows or orchards – an image that is at once confirmed when one actually sees the landscape of Normandy. Yet there is great diversity within this geographical notion.

In the Avranches area, at the outer edges of the province, crop farming has always been very important, though this part of Normandy is also well known for the fine race horses and saltmeadow lambs which are raised here. Two rivers flow through these parts: the Sée, though Avranches itself is situated on a neighbouring branch, and the Sélune, which has been turned into a long expanse of water by the dams at La Roche-qui-Boit and Vezins. Beyond that we have the River Couesnon, historically important despite its small size, marking the boundary between Normandy and Brittany, thus firmly placing Mont-Saint-Michel in Normandy. The church at Pontorson, located on the Couesnon, is said to have been founded by William the Conqueror after he had narrowly escaped drowning in the quicksands of the estuary.

Mortain is twice a border town, since it is situated on the Gance and it also separates Brittany from Maine and Normandy. The strategic importance of its location on the steep-sided tributary of the Sélune had long been put to use; but it did not really rise to prominence until William Longsword built his fortress there. This countship, which was so valuable for the province, stayed in the family, and Mortain, under Robert, the Conqueror's half brother, enjoyed a brilliant courtly life. Despite the terrible battle of August 1944, when Patton smashed

Above:
A view of the Perche Normand.

Facing page:
*Aerial view of a landscape
in the Orne Valley.*

Right:
Near Mortain, La Grande Cascade.

the counter-offensive of the German Panzers, the town has managed to retain its two main architectural attractions, both of which had been founded during the golden age of Count Robert de Mortain. Saint-Evroult, in the middle of the town, was rebuilt in the 13th century; it is a Gothic church whose dark sandstone gives it a somber appearance, somewhat tempered by the handsome belfry.

Domfront, the last outpost of the frontier along the bocage, is now merely the administrative seat of the small Passais area, though it was once the "romantic capital" of Aliénor of Aquitaine and Henri II Plantagenêt. This eagle's nest, which looks down from a height of more than two hundred feet over the Varenne Gorges, is no doubt unique in the province. The huge keep, together with the double line of enter walls, and their two dozen towers, provided an architectural setting commensurate with the queen's hotblooded temperament. That brilliant period is now a remote memory;

all that remains of the keep, which was one of the strongest in France, is a section of corner walls in the public garden, and of the fortified walls, seven towers embedded among old houses built later around them. Domfront shared the same destiny as Mortain during the Liberation, but the modern church of Saint-Julien dates from the period between the two world wars. However, the town does have one of the most interesting Romanesque buildings in the region: Notre-Dame-sur-L'Eau is a granite chapel, with a square tower, whose tranquillity may well have inspired Chrétien de Troyes to write one episode from Lancelot of the Lake. Moreover, Thomas Becket is thought to have said mass in the chapel on Christmas Day 1166. Nearby, Lonlay Abbey, also a gift from William of Bellême, who thus hoped to make amends for his ferocity, has preserved to this day its church built of a mixture of granite and the local violet-hued sandstone.

Flers-de-l'Orne, situated halfway between the Suisse Normande and Andaines Forest, is a dynamic town in a most pleasant setting, with a Renaissance château bordering on a fine park with a small lake where it is nice to go boating. The Bocage Museum in the château is devoted partly to painting and partly to regional traditions.

Facing page and above:
Saucerie Manor, at Haute-Chapelle.

Left:
A horse-breeding region…

THE SUISSE NORMANDE
AND FALAISE

With the Alabaster Coast, the Côte Fleurie and the Mancelle Alps, one is inclined to think that promotional titles devised for purposes of the tourist trade may well occasionally obscure the uniqueness of certain charming and scenic areas, besides being sometimes slightly comical.

Above and facing page:
The castle of Thury-Harcourt was burnt down in 1944. All the remains of the building are the façade and two gatelodges, but the grounds offer the visitor the compensation of a walk in a most gracious setting.

The Suisse Normande is one of these, with its rugged terrain gouged out by the Orne, its tributaries the Rouvre and the Noireau, and a host of streams which come cascading, splashing or gently rippling down wherever one looks. Here the mountains are really hills and the cliffs are mere gullies; yet the pervasive presence of water makes the Suisse Normande an oasis of calm and freshness, where one can enjoy the surprising sights to be found along the river. Leaving the Argentan Plain, the Orne forces its way through the hills of Normandy, whose hollowed relief is in fact due to the presence of the river. After a series of narrow passages

through the granite, in particular the famous escarpment of Oëtre Rock, the Orne meanders broadly before becoming once again engulfed, this time between the sandstone heights near Clécy, and then emerging on to the Caen Plain. The valley is a favourite place for excursions for the inhabitants of the regional metropolis, as it combines the charms of nature with the beauty of châteaux, mills and country inns.

The starting point for our tour is Thury-Harcourt, where all that remains of the grandiose château of the dukes of Harcourt is the porter's lodge and the large park surrounding the ruins. The most scenic loop along

the River Orne, the Boucle du Hom, is situated just outside the town, and then the valley leads to Clécy, a picturesque village combining the most attractive features of the Suisse Normande. Canoeing, rock-climbing and hang-gliding are all practised here, hikers and riders regularly cover the high ground, while the fishing is good, too, with trout and pike available in abundance. A Pont-d'Ouilly, near the confluence with the Noireau, many visitors leave the Orne in order to spend some time in this valley, in which there are numerous mills and chapels, such as Saint-Roch, at which a pardon is held each August, in full Norman dress. At Pont-Brambourg one can choose between the Louis XIII château of Saint-Sauveur and, beyond Condé-sur-Noireau, the château of Pontécoulant associated with an interesting departmental museum.

Back on the River Orne, at another confluence, this time with the Rouvre, one comes across some surprisingly rugged terrain, around the Rouvrou Bend and Oëtre Rock; these are the only places in the entire province which have anything truly mountainous about them. Further up, the road swings away from the river; indeed the Saint-Aubert Gorges can be reached only along narrow paths, such as the one that leads to the romantic ruins of the Devil's Bridge of the Jalousie Mill. Rabodanges, a short distance further on, reveals a new face of the Orne which at this point has been held in check by a dam; the artificial lake thus formed will no doubt be a great success for local tourism. There are plenty of châteaux and manors to be seen, particularly worthy of note is Repas Manor. The pleasant town of Putanges-Pont-Ecrepin, situated at the edge of this miniature version of Switzerland, is on the road to Falaise, where history brings us the loveliest of legends.

Count Robert, who was to become Duke Robert the Magnificent, used to enjoy living at the château of Falaise, as the surrounding area was rich with game. In those days he was still known as The Devil, and he indulged his two passions – women and horses – with the same domineering passion... until the day he met Arlette.

Owing to the chronicle, she was happily doing her laundry "standing among the pebbles by the fountain", in the company of young women who, like her, were also scantily clad, as it was hot. Robert, suddenly losing all his bravado, fell madly in love, and began to watch her every day from the windows of his castle. Eventually he opened his heart to Fulbert, the young beauty's father, who was a master-tanner from Falaise. Uncertain as to how to respond to such a request, as the duke, according to Viking custom still applicable in the area, could do practically as he pleased in such matters, Fulbert con-suled Arlette. She, who had never spent so much time at the fountain, asked to be driven up to the front door of the castle, dressed in all her finery, to meet the man who had chosen her. "And when the time required by Nature had passed, Arlette had a son, called William." The bastard, who was as proud as his mother, became as valiant as his father, turning this nickname into a name to be respected, one he abandoned for the title of William the Conqueror only with great regret.

William, who was loyal towards the town of his birth, embellished it and fostered its economic success, particularly by founding the Guibray horse fair, which, until its demise in the last century, was one of the most important in France. Having also made its entry into history through the front door, the town of Falaise, enriched by centuries of commerce and craftmanship, came close to leaving history as a martyr in August 1944. All the Allied armies converged on it in an attempt to encircle the German forces, leaving the town, at the end of the operation, as flattened as Caen. Restoration saved the three churches of the Trinity, Saint-Gervais and Notre-Dame-de-Guibray.

These ridges are still covered with remnants of the Celtic forest; indeed many historians are inclined to think that the Knights of the Round Table may have taken up residence in Andaines Forest, rather than in Brittany, near Paimpont. At Bagnoles-de-l'Orne such a thesis is unquestioningly accepted, and the Lancelot of the Lake Festival which takes place there each summer enjoys the distinction of being sponsored by Georges Cziffra. This event shows evidence of the new spirit of this town, whose atmosphere is moving further and further away from the mood suggested by its turn-of-the-century architecture. Together with its twin, Tessé-la-Madeleine, it tries to attract visitors outside the high season with its substantial sporting and recreational facilities. It is true, however, that its natural setting is enough to make this spa town a beautiful place. Set among pine forests punctuated here and there by spectacular outcroppings of rock, on the banks of the River Vée which widens at this point to form a small lake, Bagnoles-de-l'Orne is situated in the heart of the Normandy-Maine Regional Natural Park.

The healing powers of the waters of Bagnoles have been known for many years, as its name suggests; but the correct way to use them long remained as confidential as the simple legend which explains how they were discovered. Baron Hugues de Tessé had abandoned his old horse in Andaines Forest, as he did not want to see him die. One can only imagine how surprised he must have been on seeing that same horse come prancing back, sprightly and rejuvenated, a month later. Hugues followed the animal and found he had been bathing in a warm water spring; so he did the same and recovered the vigour of his youth. It is thought that the Baron of Bonvouloir used that same fountain of youth in order to assure himself an heir: if so, the astonishing tower of his nearby castle is a highly symbolic votive offering. Above the spa itself there are two rocky spikes known as the Saut du Capucin (Capuchin's Leap), which are named after the amazing 13-ft. leap made by a monk reinvigorated by the curative waters. The

BAGNOLES-DE-L'ORNE AND ANDAINES FOREST

The Armorican massif, which extends all around the edges of Lower Normandy, ends in one last granite and sandstone wave which protrudes near Bagnoles-de-l'Orne.

imaginative explanations devised over the years by popular wisdom have now been superseded by a more scientific judgment, which says that the water temperature is over 80 °F. – thus making it the only warm water spring in Western France – while it also has a low mineral content and some short-lived radioactive elements. These facts were uncertain when the present spa was founded. Its buildings back onto a sloping park where oaks and horse-chestnuts are sprinkled among the pines. On the other bank of the river, there are sequoias in the park of Tessé-la-Madeleine, which is also quite steep; the neo-Renaissance château of La Madeleine, now the town hall, towers over the trees, putting the final touches to a delighfully old fashioned scene.

From the 17th century onwards the forests surrounding Bagnoles-de-l'Orne were worked as a source of fuel for the glazier's ovens, the forges and the small iron ore mines in the area, while the aristocracy used them for hunting. The last wolf was killed here about the time of the establishment of the spa, but there are still wild boars and deers, hunted in grand style as the equestrian tradition is alive in these parts. A number of châteaux are situated in this most desirable area: Couteme, an unpretentious dwelling of pink brick built in 1542 by Jean de Frotté, chancellor of Margaret of Navarre, and later expanded in the 18th century with the addition of curious bell-shaped roofs. Some distance away, the château of Lassy, which towers over the town with its pepper-pot roofs, is a fine example of 15th century military architecture, complete with barbican, drawbridge, towers and high curtain walls.

Unlike Andaines Forest, the industrious town of Ferté-Macé has lost its castle, but is worth a stop for the sake of its local specialties, skewered tripe or tripe au Calvados. Near Ecouves Forest, Carrouges Castle is one of the most impressive forts in Lower Normandy. However, in fact it is not the fortress implied by its moats and its corner towers, as such brick walls with granite ties would not withstand artillery for very long. This purely residential building is apparently

named after Karl the Red, in connection with a bloody episode involving adultery which apparently took place in the original fortress on the top of the hill on which the village is situated.

Above:
Bonvouloir Tower, at Bagnoles.

Facing page, top:
*The Roc au Chien,
at Bagnoles-de-l'Orne.*

Facing page, bottom:
The Carrouges Castle.

gant and more delicate stitch which quickly gained favour among the aristocrats: the lace manufactures set up by Colbert then made Alençon lace famous throughout the courts of Europe – a fame which even survived the mechanisation of later centuries. The Conservatoire Studio for the Alençon Lace Stitch still trains women in the art of lace-making, though the secret is no longer guarded as it was once, when each worker was familiar with only one part of the famous "stitch". The former Jesuit College, founded during this period, now houses the Fine Arts and Lace Museum, where a detailed account of this saga is to be seen.

The last outcroppings of the Armorican Massif, which set the tone for Brittany and the Cotentin Peninsula, border the countryside around Alençon, underlying Perseigne Forest in the east and, north of Alençon, Ecouves Forest, where the Avaloirs Beacon, the highest point in this part of France, is situated. Made of hard rocks which have been forced into their present positions by tectonic pressures, this rugged terrain, while not rising to any great heights, nonetheless forms quite a dramatic landscape, nicely emphasized by the sparse vegetation of the Mancelles Alps. The Sarthe Valley continues after Alençon, and then, surprisingly, one finds it dashing between the sandstone rocks of the hill around the quiet villages of Saint-Pierre-des-Nids, Saint-Julien-des-Eglantiers or Saint-Léonard-des-Bois. This latter has a slightly more "alpine" feel about it, being set between the rocky escarpment of the Grand Fourché. Upstream, Saint-Céneri-le-Gérei is a blissful place which has long been beloved of painters, particularly Corot. The Romanesque church with its saddle-back roof is perched at the tip of a densely wooded promontory, overlooking the old bridge over the Sarthe and the Gothic oratory of the first hermit who succumbed to the charms of this spot. This is one's point of departure for Mount Avaloirs, perhaps a pompous-sounding name for a plateau covered with heather and young pines, though the view certainly justifies it. From the metal belvedere there is a panorama of the Perche hills.

ALENÇON CITY OF MARGUERITES

The ancient Gallo-Roman city of Alençon, near a ford across the Sarthe, would doubtless have remained a modest village, were it not for the fact that, like Falaise and Argentan, it is situated in the midst of a fertile area.

In order to prevent the success of Venetian lace from damaging the nation's finances, Colbert turned to the women of Alençon, who were famous for their skills in this field, and urged them to imitate that much-imitated Venetian stitch. One of them had just invented another more ele-

Above:
Alençon: the Préfecture.

Top and facing page: *The 15th century church, Notre-Dame of*

Alençon, is a fine example of flamboyant Gothic art. It has a particularly ornate porch, and spendid 16th century stained glass windows in the nave.

Christus   Amat   Enfantam

THE ARGENTAN COUNTRYSIDE

Before passing into the Suisse Normande, the Orne, which rises at the fort of the Perche hills, flows languidly through the gentle Argentan countryside.

This area, bordered by Ecouves Forest in the south and Gouffern Forest in the north, makes a distinct contrast with the nearby ancient rock formations, as can be seen from its architecture: from the plainest farmhouse to the most sumptuous château, here we see a blend of limestone and red brick walls, a brief transition between the timbered houses of the nearby Dives Valley and the sandstone or granite used further west. The landscape here is also a mixture of grain fields and a bocage which is famous for its studfarms. It was in the midst of this blissful countryside that the decisive engagement of the Battle of Normandy took place, when the pincer movement of the American armored units and those of Leclerc's Second Armored Division, together with the Canadian forces, closed on the ragged remnants of the German Seventh Army, on August 21st 1944.

Argentan lost in this fighting everything it had inherited from the past, with the exception of the remains of the château and the two churches of Saint-Germain and Saint-Martin, which have been laboriously saved as a result of restoration work still uncomplete to this day. Saint-Germain, which had been started in 1410, was not finished until two and a half centuries later – a fact account-

Facing page:
The countryside near Argentan.

Top and right:
Le Pin stud farm: buildings and a team of horses.

ing for the mixture of Flamboyant Gothic and Renaissance style, sometimes closely dovetailed as in the triforium and the clocktower; the choir ends in an advanced design consisting of a four-sided apse with a double ambulatory. The smaller church of Saint-Martin had a roughly similar history and great emphasis was clearly laid on both the proportions and the details of its architecture. Light enters the choir through some remarkable Renaissance stained-glass windows.

One other part of the local heritage, which had been believed lost, also survived: the Argentan stitch and the local lace, that rivaled that of Alençon. The secret of this stitch was recovered quite by chance in 1864, in an attic at the town hall, together with some parchment patterns from the golden age of lace-making. The exclusive rights to this method now belong to the nuns of the Benedictine abbey, the custodians of the lacemaking tradition, of which they present some fine examples.

Besides being responsible for the development of lace at Alençon and Argentan, Colbert also started another activity still producing spectacular results, by founding Le Pin studfarm, the pride of the Merlerault area. In 1665, after Sully had already established a stallion farm in the region, Colbert founded Le Pin as a State studfarm; Jules Hardouin-Mansart was commissioned to design a château and Le Nôtre later laid out

the terraces of this equestrian temple, which looks down over the Ure Valley. The estate nowadays is truly a preserve for regional breeding, its stables containing stallions of eight breeds, including English thoroughbreds, French trotters, Norman cobs and also Percherons, those powerful workhorses which so astonished La Varende: "Those enormous bodies, those legs, those formidable croups, those monumental shoulders, those coats whose dappled coloring makes the horse seem even bigger and younger!". The Merlerault, Gacé and Exmes areas are devoted to the raising of cattle and horses, just like Nonant-le-Pin, which has the distinction of having been the home of Alphonsine Plessis, the inspiration for La Traviata and The Lady with the Camelias.

There are also a number of superb residences in the Argentan area: Argentelles, a Renaissance manor which has been saved from ruin; Médavy, a 17th century château surrounded by fine promenades bordered with lime trees; Sassy, a century younger, set resplendently above the superb embroidery of its flowerbeds; the fortified keep at Chambois, a distinctly medieval structure; or the classical Bourg-Saint-Léonard, with its ornamental pond. They are set like fine diamonds around one of the gems of the province, the château of O. At the beginning of the 16th century this palace, on an island in the broad

stretch of water formed by the Thouanne near Mortrée, was the passion of François d'O, superintendent of finances and Governor of Paris. Sully, who was called in as his successor to reorganize the kingdom's accounts, said of it: "Even the king could not match the splendour of its carriages, its furniture and its table". In fact the lord of this particular manor died overwhelmed by debts, having spent everything on his château. The next owners continued to embellish the house, whose three wings form the most graceful of the architectural anthologies of Normandy.

From its windows, François d'O could see the spires of Sées Cathedral, in one of the oldest episcopal cities in France. A strangely serene atmosphere emanates from this pious town, whose convents, bishop's palace, seminars, museum of sacred art and lesser churches seem to escort the huge cathedral in a silent procession. This cathedral is the fifth one built in the heart of the Essay region, warfare and a series of collapses having disposed of its predecessors. The 13th century cathedral almost met the same fate because of the instability of the terrain.

Top:
The château of Médavy.

Left:
*A drawing room
in the château of Mortrée.*

Facing page, top:
Argentelles Manor.

Following pages:
*The north façade of the château
of Mortrée.*

AN ORIGINAL AREA, THE NORMAN PERCHE

"I am a Percheron, that is to say, not a Norman", said the philosopher Alain, who was born at Mortagne.

The Perche is a very special corner of the province". Finding the confines of that "corner" is no easy matter, as Maine, Normandy, Beauce and Anjou have all steadfastly claimed the Perche as their own. This was a small but rather turbulent principality, in this regard matching the great role played by the lords of Bellême or the Rotrou family, counts of Le Perche: in fact their history was quite tangled until the advent of the "gentle duke"

of Alençon, Jean II, who was also count of Le Perche. Once this companion of Joan of Arc had reconquered his domains and peace had been restored, construction proceeded at a frantic pace, using a handsome white stone with an ochre hue. Picturesque country houses replaced the castles, the churches were embellished in the Flamboyant style and a host of manor houses made their appearance on the hills, many of them later being turned into farmhouses. The fame of this distinctive region derives from many different sources, primarily from its dappled horse which has by now, unfortunately, been reduced to the status of a zoological curiosity. In the culinary sphere, pork cuts are much favoured in these parts, particularly the local favourite, back pudding, miles of which is sold at the Mortagne Fair in March. Most if not all French Canadian families derive part of their ancestry from this region and with it, apparently, they acknowledge that they have obtained from the Perche their best qualities – stability, prudence and charity.

Mortagne-au-Perche, stands guard

Above:
Farmhouse and landscape in the Perche Normande.

Top left:
The basilica of La Chapelle-Montligeon.

Facing page:
The church of St-Jean at l'Aigle.

on a rocky spur; it is the archetype of the small provincial town, with all the flavour, warmth and rustic atmosphere which that entails, in a prosperous-looking decor of watch-towers, mullioned windows and brown tiles. One unexpected sight is a Child Neptune, straddling a robust bronze horse in the gardens of the town hall. We are thus reminded that Mortagne-au-Perche is more than the domain of the Confraternity of Black Pudding Tasters.

Like all wooded areas, the Perche was a natural favorite with monks. Only one monastic community survived the Revolution in the Perche – the Grande Trappe at Soligny, near Mortagne. It was founded by Retrou III, who thereby hoped to secure eternal rest for his wife, who had been lost in the wreck of the White Ship. After a variety of misfortunes the Trappists returned to the abbey in 1814, and they still observe the strict rule of Abbot de Rancé.

The noble residences of the Perche,

from château to fortified farmhouses, probably run into the hundreds; but the manor houses, are as prominent a part of the landscape here as in Brittany, that gives this part of Normandy its special cachet. A perfect example is La Vove, with its octagonal 15th century tower and staircase turret, a decorated door and slate roof at the corner of some old farm buildings which have a very down-to-earth look about them. The manor houses are most numerous in the region of Nocé and Rémalard: for example, Courboyer, with its beautiful pepper-pot roofs covered with brown local tiles, Lormarin and La Lubinière with their three towers each; l'Angenardière, the most aristocratic of them, being graced by a charming gallery in the Italian style and a large machicolated tower flanked by a watchtower. Close by, the buildings of the former priory of Saint-Georges-de-la-Coudre are notable for their delicately decorated five-sided tower.

Left:
At Conches-en-Houche, the ruins of a medieval towe.

Bottom:
The church of Tillières-sur-Avre.

Facing page:
The Avre, near Verneuil.

On its way through Chartres, the last of these moves outside the region for a while: that was the river, the Avre, chosen by a young and realistic King and a Viking whose ambitions did not allow him to stay within the Epte boundary. The modest river, which was thus closely involved in the birth of the duchy of Normandy in 911, has since retained that role, sometimes by military means, until the peace and tranquillity of today, when its waters merely separate the two regions.

Verneuil-sur-Avre was an integral part of that line of moats, as its layout testifies.

The Madeleine Tower is the soul of this city, especially as it adjoins an original Romanesque nave which is so stark and plain that in another setting it might be mistaken for a tithe barn, although that initial impression is offset by the handsome Gothic choir. The tower, four stories tall, is crowned by a twin stone diadem which is definitely similar to the Butter Tower of Rouen Cathedral. It was, moreover, financed in exactly the same way – with the proceeds of Lenten dispensations. Like its prestigious cousin, the Madeleine Tower caries an abundance of statues, while the interior of the church is also richly adorned, with stained glass and superb decorative work of the 15th and 16th centuries. From the outside the church of Notre-Dame, closer to the Avre, is a rather nondescript Romanesque structure, while its interior is a genuine museum with an excellent collection of statues from the early 16th century. Lastly the Grise Tower, so named because of the hard limestone (grison) of its thick walls, is all that remains of the castle of Henri Beauclerc – a cylindrical keep quite unlike the angular buttressed towers customary of that period.

THE AVRE VALLEY, FRONTIER OF THE FORMER DUCHY

The numerous rivers in the Perche hills flow in every direction: the Sarthe and the Huisne towards the Loire; the Orne, the Dives, the Touques and the Risle, towards the Seine Bay; and the Iton and the Avre discharge into the Eure, which itself flows down from the same high ground.

In the vicinity of Verneuil there are some fine churches, such as Pullay and Cintray, and a number of châteaux. Of these, Chambray is the most majestic, whereas the three noble dwellings at Condé-sur-Iton are certainly the most original, with their juxtaposition of Renaissance, classical period and modern style, further enhanced by a beautiful park. However, history was not made and unmade on the River Iton, so we must return to the Avre and the Eure in order to follow the old Norman frontier.

Nonancourt was fortified from 1112 onwards by Henri I; next to the Flamboyant church of Saint-Martin, one can still see the remains of the castle where Richard Lionheart and Philippe-Auguste laid down the terms for their joint involvement in the Third Crusade. Through the efforts of Richard II of Normandy, Tillières-sur-Avre had been on the defensive line a whole century previously, and here again a tower and a gate of the old castle are still standing. This town also bears the imprint of the ecclesiastical dynasty of Le Veneur, and the church of Saint-Hilaire, built on a Romanesque base which one of them remodeled in 1546, is noteworthy for its choir and an adjoining chapel.

After the confluence with the Eure, the last historically important place in the region is certainly Ivry-la-Bataille, where the Ligueurs of Mayenne were crushed in 1590 – an event Henry IV made famous with his call: "Rally round my white plume!"

Left:
Verneuil-sur-Avre: the church of La Madeleine.

Right:
A 16th century window.

A SURVIVING CITY: EVREUX

Evreux, which lies calm and refreshed in the arms of the River Iton, not far from the capital, is a good place to stop on a tour of Normandy.

However, that very proximity and the strategic importance of the Eure Valley, into which the Iton soon flows, have brought the town a stream of calamities since the earliest times. Excavations have shown that old Evreux, slightly to the east on the plateau, was already an important town when it was sacked by the Vandals; then the Roman city, ringed by hills, ancestor of the modern Evreux, shared the good fortunes of the Empire behind its enormous ramparts. The Franks under Clovis occupied Evreux, which then began to be evangelized; but Rollo looted it in 897. One century later the town became the seat of a Norman county: the King of France, who supported Count Henri Beauclerc, laid it waste in 1119. Taking advantage of the fact that his brother Richard Lionheart was in captivity, Landless John sold Evreux to Philippe-Auguste; however, on learning that Richard had been set free, he massacred the three hundred French members of the garrison and returned the fort to his brother. Enraged by such treachery, Philippe-Auguste laid siege to the town and eventually regained possession of it, having all the English soldiers and all the townspeople executed, before burning the place down.

The misfortunes of this gentle city began once again in the Hundred Years' War: the most famous of the Counts of Evreux, Charles the Bad, King of Navarre and pretender to the throne of France, took it successively into the French and the English camps, before John the Good seized it and also burnt it down. Twenty years later in 1378, Du Guesdin returned Evreux to the crown, but the city was ruined by yet another fire. It was not until 1441, when Robert de Flouques captured it one more time from the English that the serenity of this county seat was restored. Many years later, during the Revolution, six churches, two convents and two abbeys were razed to the ground. And finally, in 1940 and 1944, bombs and shells came crashing on Evreux, which burnt for a whole week. Notwithstanding its past, Evreux is a sprightly place, with plenty of flowers and shade, around its surviving architectural gems – the cathedral, the former bishop's palace, the belfry and the church of Saint-Taurin.

The cathedral of Notre-Dame, the symbolic prize of each battle, is anything but homogeneous, and parts of it were rebuilt at varying times from the 12th to the 17th century. Nevertheless, its various components, in a light-coloured stone, do combine harmoniously to form an elegant whole. The base of the nave dates from the time of Henry Beauclerc, whom Pope Calixtus II compelled to rebuild what he had destroyed; however, that 12th century nave, which was burnt once again, was not reconstructed until 1253. Later on the choir was enlarged, but fate was very unkind to the cathedral, which did not enter its golden age until the reign of Louis XI, a most generous monarch towards the town; the transept, the lantern-tower known as the Silver Belfry (Clocher d'Argent) and the superbly limpid stained-glass windows, among the finest in France, all date, accordingly, from the end of the 14th century. The north doorway, an outstanding example of Flamboyant design, was completed in 1504 and the remarkable wood screens of the chapels in the ambulatory were added in the 16th century. The final phase of building brought the façade towers, decorated in the style of Henry II. In the 17th century the final touch was

Above:
The mill at Cocherel.

Top left:
Evreux: the cathedral and the museum.

Facing page:
The church of Pacy-sur-Eure.

put to the cathedral, which is still being restored today, in the form of Le Gros-Pierre (Big Stone), as the north tower was affectionately nicknamed.

The old bishop's palace, also much affected by history, and now housing a museum, has also had its Gothic glory restored, and can bear comparison with its counterparts in Beauvais and Rouen. One of its rooms, located underground, borders on the original ramparts, which make a perfect setting for collections dating back to the early years of the Christian era. The elegant 15th century clocktower, La Louise, with its great bell weighing two tons, luckily escaped damage during the war. The church of Saint-Taurin, rather eccentrically situated at the end of the rue Josephine – a reminder that Evreux was made a duchy for the spurned empress – deserves to be visited on account of its magnificent stained-glass windows, and particularly for the reliquary of the saint after whom it is named. This masterpiece of the 13th century, made of enamelled silver and gilded copper in the form of a miniature Sainte-Chapelle, is one of the most beautiful specimens known of craftsmanship.

The Eure Valley, to which Evreux can rightly be considered to belong, has for many years been one of the major axes of trade and communication in Normandy, and, at the same time, practically at the gates of the capital, a sort of highly attractive version of the Loire Valley. After the fighting between England and France, lavish country houses were built in the midst of the delightful scenery along the banks of the river: Saint-Georges-Notel and its large park; the illustrious Anet, on the Ile-de-France side of the river; La Folletière at Neuilly; Breuilpont, Chambray, Heudreville, and also the delightful Acquigny, all agreeably soften, with their refinement, the forbidding impression left by the fortresses which were built along the frontiers, the Epte and the Avre, during the provinces early years.

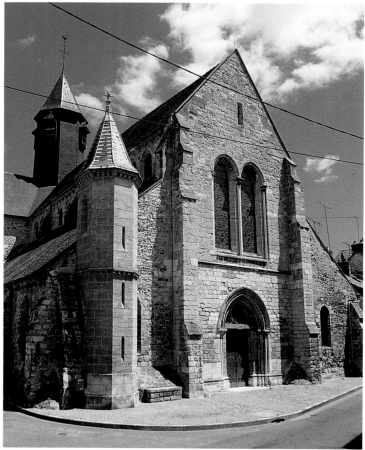

Achevé d'imprimer en novembre 1998
sur les presses de l'imprimerie Bona à Turin
Imprimé en Italie
Dépôt légal : novembre 1998
ISBN: 2-8307-0131-3